New Directions for
Adult and Continuing
Education

Susan Imel
Jovita M. Ross-Gordon
COEDITORS-IN-CHIEF

Adult Education in an Urban Context

Problems, Practices, and
Programming for
Inner-City Communities

Larry G. Martin
Elice E. Rogers
EDITORS

D1522268

Number 101 • Spring 2004
Jossey-Bass
San Francisco

ADULT EDUCATION IN AN URBAN CONTEXT: PROBLEMS, PRACTICES, AND
PROGRAMMING FOR INNER-CITY COMMUNITIES
Larry G. Martin, Elice E. Rogers (eds.)
New Directions for Adult and Continuing Education, no. 101
Susan Imel, Jovita M. Ross-Gordon, Coeditors-in-Chief

Microfilm copies of issues and articles are available in 16mm and 35mm
as well as microfiche in 105mm, through University Microfilms Inc., 300
North Zeeb Road, Ann Arbor, Michigan 48106-1346.

NEW DIRECTIONS FOR ADULT AND CONTINUING EDUCATION (ISSN 1052-
2891, electronic ISSN 1536-0717) is part of The Jossey-Bass Higher and
Adult Education Series and is published quarterly by Wiley Subscription
Services, Inc., A Wiley company, at Jossey-Bass, 989 Market Street, San
Francisco, California 94103-1741. Periodicals Postage Paid at San Fran-
cisco, California, and at additional mailing offices. POSTMASTER: Send
address changes to New Directions for Adult and Continuing Education,
Jossey-Bass, 989 Market Street, San Francisco, California, 94103-1741.

SUBSCRIPTIONS cost $80.00 for individuals and $160.00 for institutions,
agencies, and libraries.

EDITORIAL CORRESPONDENCE should be sent to the Coeditors-in-Chief,
Susan Imel, ERIC/ACVE, 1900 Kenny Road, Columbus, Ohio 43210-1090.
e-mail: imel.l@osu.edu, or Jovita M. Ross-Gordon, Southwest Texas State
University, EAPS Dept., 601 University Drive, San Marcos, TX 78666.

Cover photograph by Jack Hollingsworth © Photodisc

www.josseybass.com

CONTENTS

EDITORS' NOTES

The urban context is defined by several features that shape the character and structure of adult education practice: housing market discrimination, residential segregation, social isolation and economic transformation of low-income neighborhoods, racioethnic population density, segregated K-12 schools, the evolution of alternative language structures, and other elements. These features have led to the development of a bifurcated system of service delivery of adult education programs targeting learners who are either resource rich or resource poor. These programs are typically organized around the presumed needs of potential learners based on their race or ethnicity, socioeconomic standing, geographical location, or some combination thereof. This sourcebook provides insight into urban adult education practice by analyzing urban context issues, problems, policies, and programs, particularly as these affect residents of low-income communities.

The first four chapters situate adult education within the urban context. In Chapter One, Larry G. Martin defines the term *urban* and considers the historical evolution of urban centers, urban context barriers to adult education, and opportunities for the creation of innovative programs that focus on the unique learning needs of urban residents. In Chapter Two, Elice E. Rogers and Catherine A. Hansman explicate the problems that adult education practitioners confront in assisting residents of low-income urban communities to access and utilize educational opportunities. In Chapter Three, Tonette S. Rocco and Suzanne J. Gallagher examine the nature and importance of discriminative justice. They provide an analysis of discrimination that can assist adult educators in constructing knowledge about privilege, oppression, and justice in urban adult education. Chapter Four, by Talmadge C. Guy, utilizes the concept of the city as educational agent to explore the ways in which the city's racialized structure influences the cultural production, commodification, and consumption of African American popular culture, especially as exemplified through hip-hop and "gangsta" rap music as the dominant form of black urban cultural expression.

The last four chapters address the issue of responsive programming for urban adult learners. Chapter Five, by E. Paulette Isaac and Martha Strittmatter Tempesta, considers how responsive community programming assists urban learners in revitalizing their communities. The authors examine two community-based organizations that are effectively creating positive changes in local neighborhoods via collaborative strategies for the delivery of educational programming. In Chapter Six, Daniel T. Norris and Simone Conceição examine the factors contributing to the digital divide in adult education. They then present opportunities for adult educators to narrow the digital divide in low-income, urban communities. Chapter Seven, by Patricia Leong Kappel and Barbara J. Daley, explores transformational learning theory as it is applied to low-income urban learners. It identifies the elements of the theory that are necessary for facilitating transformative learning among urban adult populations. Finally, Chapter Eight by Larry G. Martin and Elice E. Rogers presents new directions for urban adult education.

We believe that by combining practice with research, theory, and policy, this text provides an insightful and much needed resource to adult education practitioners in academic, community, and work-related urban settings.

Larry G. Martin
Elice E. Rogers
Editors

LARRY G. MARTIN is professor of adult and continuing education at the University of Wisconsin–Milwaukee.

ELICE E. ROGERS is assistant professor of adult learning and development at Cleveland State University.

1

Context is vitally important for urban adult education because it tends to create physical, psychological, and sociocultural distance between and among learners and various providers of adult and continuing education programs, thereby creating barriers and the differential provision of adult learning opportunities for some urban populations.

Adult Education in the Urban Context

Larry G. Martin

The urban context represents the social and environmental situations that inform the lived experiences of individuals, groups, and communities that reside in densely populated urban areas. These everyday experiences differ for adult learners based on their sociodemographic characteristics, such as age (or life-stage), income and socioeconomic standing, occupation (or work situation), and other factors. Context is vitally important for urban adult education because it tends to create physical, psychological, and sociocultural distance between and among learners and various providers of adult and continuing education programs, thereby creating barriers and the differential provision of adult learning opportunities for some urban populations. This chapter explores the historical characteristics of the urban context that help to shape the form, content, and scope of adult education programs in urban areas, particularly as these characteristics affect inner-city communities. Several topics are discussed: the definition of *urban,* the historical evolution of urban centers, urban context and barriers to adult education, and urban adult education programs.

Definition of *Urban*

A confusing array of ideas and concepts is associated with the word *urban.* The term *city* has been used in lieu of *urban* to designate a specific geographic space that has been identified as a unit of government. For example, our nation's largest cities include New York, Los Angeles, Houston, and Chicago. Additionally, some observers prefer to use the term *metropolitan* as a substitute for *urban.* For example, Greer (1989) suggests that the center and the periphery are crude ways of separating the urbane component of metropolitan areas. He observes that the metropolitan area may best be seen

NEW DIRECTIONS FOR ADULT AND CONTINUING EDUCATION, no. 101, Spring 2004 © Wiley Periodicals, Inc.

as the city, with its dense urban center and its tall towers, surrounded by a seemingly endless spread of suburban housing.

In contrast to this geographic definition, *density* is the primary attribute used by the U.S. Census Bureau to classify the nation's urban population. Census 2000 defined *urban* as all territory, population, and housing units located within an urbanized area (UA) or an urban cluster (UC) (U.S. Census Bureau, 2002). It delineated UA and UC boundaries to encompass densely settled territory that consists of *core census block groups,* or blocks that have a population density of at least a thousand people per square mile, and *surrounding census blocks,* which have an overall density of at least five hundred people per square mile. In addition, it observed that under certain conditions, less densely settled territory may be part of each UA or UC. In this definition, geographic entities, such as census tracts, counties, metropolitan areas, and the territory outside of metropolitan areas, are often split between urban and rural territory, and the population and housing units they contain are often partly classified as urban and partly classified as rural.

The term *urban* is also often used interchangeably with the term *inner city.* However, the terms *inner city* and *central city* are often used interchangeably and typically refer to densely populated low-income neighborhoods located in cities that are dominated by racial and ethnic minorities. In this chapter, the term *urban* recognizes the population density attribute described by the U.S. Census Bureau. However, much of the focus is on a much more targeted geographic area called the *inner city.* This perspective recognizes that urban areas represent densely populated urban centers dominated by skyscrapers that symbolize the tremendous wealth and prosperity of some urban dwellers, yet they stand in sharp contrast and are often in proximity to inner-city communities that are sometimes populated by the poorest of the poor. Both of these communities share an economic relationship with the wealthy and highly educated residents of surrounding suburbs. The case of Milwaukee's Little Beirut captures many of the socioeconomic and educational struggles faced by inner-city residents.

Little Beirut: The Struggle of Inner-City Communities

Little Beirut is a thirteen-block area that constitutes one of the youngest and poorest neighborhoods in the city of Milwaukee (McBride and Ortiz, 2002). To some in the community, it is considered a survival zone that is reckless and rootless. Named because of its history of frequent and violent encounters between residents and police and narcotics officers, its drug-related crimes, and its lack of employment opportunities, Little Beirut epitomizes Wilson's (1987) depiction of a "hypoghettoized" community. McBride and Ortiz (2002), reporters from the *Milwaukee Journal Sentinel,* have provided a profile of the community. They find that the U.S. Census indicates that the community's median household income in 1999 was $15,192 compared to $32,216 for the rest of the city. Its racial makeup was 96.3 percent African

American and 2.3 percent white (versus 38 percent and 52 percent respectively for the city). More than one-third of the households were headed by single mothers with children (compared to about 14 percent for the city) and approximately 22 percent were receiving public assistance (compared to about 5 percent for the city). The unemployment rate in 2000 was 20.3 percent (compared to 6 percent for the city). In regard to education, 56 percent of adults had earned a high school diploma (compared to about 75 percent for the city) and only 3 percent had earned a bachelor's degree (compared to about 18 percent for the city).

The community received national attention with the beating death of Charlie Young, a thirty-six-year-old African American man. His death was a tragic and symbolic incident that captured in one moment the catastrophic and complex circumstances that envelop some residents of central cities throughout the United States. The incident occurred during an October Sunday night. Newspaper accounts filed by Abdul-Alim and McBride (2002) have attempted to reconstruct the incident. Accordingly, at about 10 P.M., a group of African American youth were "hanging out" together when an intoxicated Young intruded on a game of "insults" between a thirteen-year-old boy and his girlfriend. The boy apparently threw an egg that hit Young on the shoulder. The six-foot-two, two-hundred-pound Young retaliated by chasing down the thirteen-year-old, knocking him to the pavement, and kicking him. At that point a fourteen-year-old boy became involved in the confrontation by throwing a baby stroller into Young. Witnesses indicated that Young then "flashed a knife" at the fourteen-year-old. The boys tried to "disarm" him. During the struggle, Young punched the fourteen-year-old in the mouth, knocking him unconscious and dislodging a tooth. Young then ran away, seeking safety in the neighborhood, with the boys in pursuit. The boys, including some members of a street gang, gathered up other boys and older males in the neighborhood. Young sought safety by hiding in a nearby empty lot. The hunt and chase lasted about forty-five minutes. In an effort to escape his pursuers, Young ran inside a duplex, from where he was dragged out and bludgeoned into a coma. The attackers struck Young fifty to sixty times with an assortment of makeshift weapons, such as a mop handle, a shovel, folding chairs, bats, a rake, a tree limb, and others. Charlie Young died of his injuries two days later. Eleven boys (ages ten to seventeen) and three adult males (ages nineteen to thirty-three) were arrested and tried for the beating death (Rybarczyk, 2003).

As political officials and community leaders tried to make sense of the senseless beating and the ruined lives of not only the victim but also the perpetrators of the crime, some details regarding the attackers emerged. According to Barton (2002), these African American males represented the overall demographics of their community. Several attended school and received average grades, while others had discontinued school or received poor grades. About three of them were affiliated with street gangs, and four others had previous criminal convictions for trespassing, burglary, possession of a nine-millimeter handgun, violating curfew, and other offenses. An eighteen-year-old was described as being able to "read and write a little" (p. 16A). He "prints his name in a childlike hand" (p. 16A). A sixteen-year-old was described as having a learning disability that made it difficult for him to read and write (Barton, 2002). A fourteen-year-old was described as having an IQ of fifty-six and as being the father of a baby girl. Most of the boys were being reared in single-parent homes. Three had lost their fathers to acts of violence or had dads who were incarcerated for criminal behavior. As these individuals passed through the criminal justice system, the great majority of them were processed as adults and received considerable time in prison. Most pleaded guilty to reckless homicide. Sentences ranged from eighteen months to eighteen years. The ten-year-old was not charged because he was found incompetent to stand trial (Rybarczyk, 2003). In addition, Young's mother won a $1,029 million judgment against almost all the defendants, and the defendants' parents were held financially liable ("Young Mother Awarded $1 Million," 2003). According to figures compiled by the *Milwaukee Journal Sentinel,* it will cost $2.7 million to bring the defendants to justice; that is, it will cost $176.05 for each day spent in a juvenile prison and $71.19 a day for adult prison.

Little Beirut epitomizes the problems and issues faced by residents of central cities in America: street gangs, interpersonal violence, drug addiction, struggling and failing K-12 schools, enduring poverty, single-parent homes, welfare dependence, black-on-black crime, teenage pregnancy, unemployment, homelessness, low-literacy, learning and other types of disabilities, and other problems (Wilson, 1987; Hacker, 1992). Although this case is not representative of all U.S. cities or metropolitan areas, it does capture the reality of far too many inner-city communities in the nation's most cerebrated cities. It provides graphic imagery of the anger and hair-trigger frustration experienced by the youngest residents. It also details the human and social costs of societal neglect of such communities. Communities like Little Beirut manifest a complex and difficult array of sociostructural issues and problems that morph into educational and learning needs as city leaders and inner-city communities seek solutions. From the sociostructural viewpoint, however, one must ask, How has this country evolved a system that has produced an urban space like Little Beirut? What decisions have government agencies, private industries, and private citizens made that have contributed to the creation of such urban spaces? An analysis of the history of the U.S. urban system suggests that it has evolved in several phases.

The Historical Evolution of Urban Centers

Characterized today by their massive office towers, large convention and cultural centers, and attractive shopping malls, contemporary urban centers are also marked by images of despair (Bender, 2003) that are captured in the Little Beirut case. These images, however, represent realities that have evolved over time as American cities have taken shape on this country's landscape. Bender (2003) describes five periods of development for cities and urban areas: predominately rural, the walking city, early divisionalization, full specialization, and decentralization (that is, the modern city).

At its inception under the Constitution, the United States was a *predominately rural* (95 percent) and agricultural society (Bender, 2003). The initial period of development of the American urban system occurred as new settlements, such as Jamestown in 1607, were founded on the Atlantic seaboard (Eyesberg, 1989). A vast network of cities developed in the United States during the course of the nineteenth century. This growth was driven by a dynamic economy, improvements in transportation systems, and increases in immigration. By 1920 the urban population exceeded the rural population (Bender, 2003).

The late-eighteenth-century city was considered a *walking city*—that is, a comfortable walk represented the limits of human movement and thereby affected urban culture. Until the middle of the nineteenth century, people and messages moved at the same speed because urban life was not easily managed over a territory exceeding more than a mile or two from the center. In such cities there was no strictly residential district, nor was there one exclusively devoted to business. Residential segregation by class and ethnicity was limited. Employees often lived in the same houses as their employers or in a rear building (Bender, 2003).

In the middle decades of the nineteenth century, *divisionalization* characterized many cities. In 1850, the city was significantly influenced by changes in communication and transportation, enhanced trade, increased urbanization, growth in manufacturing, and increases in the number of native migrants and foreign immigrants. These changes produced a multiplicity of specialized environments, such as distinct commercial areas, manufacturing enterprises, working-class neighborhoods, heavy industrial enterprises, major financial institutions, entertainment establishments, fashionable neighborhoods, and slums. These changes also led to the separation of work and residence. With the breakdown of the traditional apprentice system, work groups increased in size, and most employees became wage earners for life. These employees formed a working class that sought out cheap housing of their own, and employers tended to move away from the workplace to exclusively residential areas that better sustained a developing interest in domesticity (Bender, 2003).

From 1890 to 1945 the full specialization of urban space was achieved through changes in the physical form of cities—for example, the introduction of elevators facilitated vertical movement in the form of tall buildings, and horizontal movement was induced as cities extended outward from their central business core (Bender, 2003). These changes were accompanied by changes in social composition. Although African Americans had lived in cities as early as the colonial period, after 1890 and especially during World Wars I and II, black migration to northern cities accelerated, driven by southern racism, changes in the conditions and technology of southern agriculture, and perceived opportunities in the North. Also in the 1890s, the volume and source of foreign immigration changed as large numbers of immigrants from eastern and southern Europe came to the United States, settling mainly in cities. Neighborhoods defined by class, race, and ethnicity evolved.

After World War II, a series of socioeconomic and policy changes led to the evolution of the *modern city*. The automobile and the freeway system that was made possible by the Federal Highway Act of 1956 encouraged decentralization that undermined the central city. Concurrently, the Federal Housing Administration, the GI Bill, and the tax system made purchasing a home easier, opening suburban living to large numbers of middle and working-class people (Bender, 2003), thereby creating urban sprawl. Changes in Affirmative Action policies and in laws prohibiting discrimination on the basis of race and ethnicity also paved the way for minorities in central-city neighborhoods to relocate to suburban communities. Therefore, during the 1970s and 1980s the urban landscape evolved community enclaves based on race, ethnicity, and income as central-city communities experienced a steady out-migration of middle- and working-class families. During this period, inner-city communities experienced what Wilson (1987, p. 58) describes as "concentration effects" that resulted from the social transformation and social isolation of their communities. These communities were left without a social buffer and thereby experienced prolonged increases in joblessness, which created a ripple effect of social isolation that excluded them from the job network system that permeated other neighborhoods and that is important in learning about or being recommended for jobs that become available in various parts of the city. In addition, as prospects for employment diminished, other alternatives, such as welfare and the underground economy, became a way of life (Wilson, 1987). Girls who became pregnant out of wedlock invariably gave birth, because of a shrinking pool of marriageable—that is, employed—black males (Wilson, 1987). Today, in the form of Little Beirut, we see the residual effects of two decades of social, economic, and educational policies that have failed to address the needs of inner-city communities.

Large cities today, such as New York, Los Angeles, and Miami, are now being transformed into world cities by a new wave of immigration from Asia, Latin America, the Caribbean, and Africa (Bender, 2003). They are also sites of global economic development efforts as cities attempt to utilize their strategic asset (that is, massive human resources) as raw materials in the new global economy. Education is described in this context as a regionally defining resource that has global implications for the local economy (Blakely, 1997). As demonstrated in the case of Little Beirut, however, the inner-city communities of these cities are plagued by intergenerational poverty and the concomitant issues associated with lack of educational attainment and differential access to adult and continuing education programs. The issues facing these communities must be addressed if urban areas are to utilize fully their human resources as strategic assets.

Urban Context Barriers to Adult Education

Modern urban centers share several sociostructural characteristics that affect the type and quality of adult education that is provided to the various individuals and communities that reside within their borders. A primary characteristic is the interlocking pattern of racial and income discrimination that has become synonymous with urban living. This discriminatory practice is most noticeable in residential segregation that is driven by a mutually reinforcing chain of events: white racial prejudice, housing market discrimination, labor market discrimination, and resulting interracial economic disparities (Galster and Keeney, 1988; Wilson, 1987).

White Racial Prejudice and Housing Market Discrimination. Galster and Keeney (1988) observe that white racial prejudice is reflected in the decisions of individuals, families, employers, and communities regarding the extent to which they will affiliate with individuals and groups that differ from them in race and ethnicity. In urban communities, the effects of racial prejudice are most pronounced in the housing market discrimination that has resulted from differential treatment of clientele by housing market agents who may discriminate out of fear of reaction from the prejudiced white clientele they serve (Galster and Keeney, 1988). A measure of white prejudice has been observed by Hacker (1992), who indicates that most American cities have neighborhoods whose residents are largely working and almost exclusively white. He observes that most of these enclaves have endeavored to preserve their character by doing everything necessary—such as committing arson, firing guns, and using other means of intimidation—to ensure that black families will not move in. Also, until the passage of the federal Fair Housing Act in 1968, this form of discrimination was so ingrained in American culture that the federal government itself redlined in the granting of home mortgages under the Federal Housing Administration and Veterans Administration, enforced racially restrictive covenants on deeds in new subdivisions, funded racially segregated housing projects, and supported urban renewal projects that displaced low-income residents (Quinn and Pawasarat, 2003). Although Galster and Keeney (1988) note that the existence of such discrimination has been well documented, a recent study by the U.S. Department of Housing and Urban Development (Turner, Ross, Galster, and Yingy, 2002) found significant levels of racial and ethnic discrimination in both the rental and the sales markets of urban areas nationwide. Their study of 4,600 paired tests (that is, with one racial minority applicant and one white homeseeker) in twenty-three metropolitan areas nationwide uncovered countless instances of illegal discrimination against minority homeseekers. This type of discriminatory practice is problematic because it raises the costs of the search for housing, creates barriers to homeownership and housing choice, and contributes to the perpetuation of residential segregation.

Residential Segregation. Housing market discrimination produces residential segregation of neighborhoods on the basis of race, ethnicity, and income. Sociologists have tracked residential segregation via an analysis of segregation indexes since the 1950s (Quinn and Pawasarat, 2003). The historic dissimilarity segregation index most commonly used today to rank metropolitan areas and cities as to their degree of segregation was first published in 1965. *Segregation* was defined as the lack of an even distribution of the black population. Ideally, no neighborhood would be all black or all white, and each race would be represented in each neighborhood in approximately the same proportion as in the city as a whole.

Quinn and Pawasarat (2003) utilized 2000 Census data to examine residential segregation in the one hundred largest metropolitan areas in the United States. They created a new index that used city blocks compared to census tracts as the unit of analysis. They found that most metropolitan areas are still highly segregated. Blacks living on blocks with a predominantly (over 80 percent) black population made up 41.3 percent of blacks population in the largest metropolitan areas. Nearly a fourth (23.4 percent) of blacks lived on black-white integrated blocks, and 21.7 percent of blacks lived on a remaining category of blocks with Latino, Asian, or other populations as well as whites in a variety of combinations. Another 13.6 percent lived on majority white (more than 50 percent) blocks where they constituted less than a fifth of the block's population. Conversely, whites living on blocks with a predominantly (more than 80 percent) white population made up 66.4 percent of the total white population in the one hundred largest metropolitan areas, while 26.5 percent of whites lived on blocks with other population mixtures, such as Latinos and Asians as well as blacks, in a variety of combinations. About 6.5 percent of whites lived on black-white integrated blocks. A small proportion of whites (0.6 percent) lived on majority black (more than 50 percent) blocks, where they constituted less than a fifth of the block's population.

In addition, Hacker (1992) suggests that race- and ethnicity-related residential segregation is correlated to family income when he observed that two-thirds of poor white Americans live in suburbs or rural areas. Their homes, however, are less likely to be clustered together in slum neighborhoods. Among the poor white families who do live in urban areas, less than a quarter reside in low-income tracts, which suggests that there are few white ghettos. Urban black families below the poverty line are more visibly segregated. About 70 percent of such households are concentrated in low-income neighborhoods. Residential segregation works to create enclaves of communities based on race, ethnicity, income, and concomitant values and perspectives.

Social Isolation and Economic Transformation. Another by-product of segregated housing is social isolation. As indicated earlier, central-city communities became socially isolated during the 1970s and 1980s. During this period cities were transformed from centers of production and distribution of goods to centers of administration, finance, and information exchange. Blue-collar jobs were replaced in part by knowledge-intensive white-collar jobs requiring employees, such as managers, professionals, and high-level technical and administrative personnel, to have educational credentials, excluding those who had less than a high school diploma. Also, industrial plants experienced decentralization and the flight of manufacturing jobs abroad, to the Sunbelt states, or to the suburbs (Kasarda, 1989; Wilson, 1987).

As a consequence, inner-city communities were plagued by massive joblessness, flagrant and open lawlessness, and low-achieving schools. The residents of these areas, whether women and children of welfare families or aggressive street criminals, tended to become socially isolated from mainstream patterns of behavior (Wilson, 1987). As residential discrimination declined for prosperous minority families, the forced community of the ethnic enclave lost its best-educated residents to middle-class, often integrated communities (Greer, 1989). The leadership roles were depleted, and valuable sources of information were lost. Therefore, inner-city communities were left with an increasingly economically impoverished racially and ethnically diverse minority population. Greer (1989) suggests that the socioeconomic and cultural processes that have produced urban spaces like Little Beirut tend to become self-sealing: the neighborhood inhabitants' sources of information become only those who are much like themselves; blacks, Hispanics, and whites of each specific class tend to associate socially only with those who are of their own class; and children growing up in these communities are forced to attend largely segregated K-12 schools.

Segregated Schools and Alternative Language Structures. Segregated housing patterns in urban communities have resulted in segregated K-12 schools. It is not uncommon for urban school children to attend schools in which racial minorities constitute more than 50 percent of the student population. For example, Freeman, Brookhart, and Loadman (1999) observe that during the 1990–1991 school year, 119,539 African American students attended one of Chicago's 203 segregated African American schools, in which African American children comprised 99 to 100 percent of the student population. During the same year, 4,903 Hispanic youngsters attended one of eight segregated Hispanic schools in Chicago. These schools represented more than 40 percent of all elementary schools in the Chicago system. Most racially, ethnically, or linguistically diverse schools share three common characteristics: the majority of students come from low-income families, students' academic performance on standardized tests typically falls below state and national norms, and student mobility rates and absenteeism are high. One of the effects of attending underperforming inner-city schools in racially and ethnically segregated communities is an acceptance of alternative language structures.

Segregated communities and the social isolation of community enclaves have given rise to alternative language structures in urban areas. Greer (1989) argues that behaviors that would be rare, disliked, and highly visible in nonurban settings are more commonplace, better organized, and often less stigmatized in cities. These observations seem to capture the language experiences of African Americans and other language minorities in inner-city communities. For example, Flowers (2000) has observed that because of the differences between the African American dialect and standard English, the schooling of blacks in the United States has negated their language, lived experiences, and culture. The language used among African Americans has historically been characterized as deviant, deficient, and different. Flowers examined black dialect usage and its function among African American learners in urban adult basic education programs. One of her findings was that the African American adult students did not consider the way they spoke as being different or distinct from standard English. When asked about and given examples of standard, black, or slang language, some referred to black English as standard English and to standard English as black English. They therefore saw no difference between the two language systems. The students did distinguish, however, between black English, standard English, and slang. Adult learners who experience difficulty distinguishing between an alternative language system and the dominant language system will likely experience difficulty in a mainstream labor market that views alternative language systems as deviant.

Labor Market Discrimination. As adults, the minority residents of inner-city communities may face labor market discrimination as they seek employment and economic advancement. This form of discrimination results from employers who may act on their personal prejudices to discriminate against minority workers in the realms of hiring, promotion, retention, and wages. They may also discriminate in response to the prejudices of their existing white workers (or of the customers who must interface with these workers) to avoid interracial tensions in the workplace that might prove deleterious to productivity (or to sales) (Galster and Keeney, 1988). Hacker (1992) argues that, unlike in previous years, absolute barriers to employment have been broken, and every occupation has some blacks among its practitioners. In many areas the numbers remain exceedingly small. For example, Hacker (1992) observes that blacks remain underrepresented in the professions of engineering, law, medicine, architecture, journalism, and others. They are overrepresented, however, in jobs that whites are reluctant to take, such as hotel maids, nursing aids, correctional officers, postal clerks, janitors and cleaners, and others. Blacks seem to be well represented in several occupations, such as, insurance adjusters, bankers, garage workers, chemical technicians, and others.

Given the social isolation experienced by inner-city residents, and the inability of inner-city schools to prepare students for a productive work life, Galster and Keeney (1988) argue that interracial economic disparities (that is, differences in occupational attainment, earnings, and so on) between minorities and whites can be explained at the metropolitan level by interracial differences in the profiles of personal attributes (such as educational attainment and other basic skills, problem-solving ability, decision making, dependability, positive attitude, cooperativeness, and other affective skills and traits) that are evaluated by the labor market, in conjunction with structural features of the market that shape how these attributes are measured. Such disparities will be exacerbated when labor market discrimination serves to undervalue whatever human capital the minority workforce possesses. Residents of inner-city communities are therefore caught in a web of mutually reinforcing barriers that significantly inhibit their efforts. Adult and continuing education programs could represent a viable resource to these residents.

Urban Adult Education Programs

In urban centers new and previously unknown forms of learning opportunities have emerged, from innovative partnership arrangements with previously unaffiliated organizations to the targeting of specialized groups of learners that can be found in critical masses only in urban areas. In most urban centers, however, the adult and continuing education enterprise has evolved into a bifurcated system to meet the learning and educational needs of urban learners.

Programs Targeting Resource-Rich Communities. For middle class adults and their families from predominately white and racially integrated communities, the urban landscape currently offers numerous opportunities for a wide variety of both general and highly specialized learning programs. Numerous providers have evolved in these areas to take advantage of the critical mass of urban populations. These providers are able to exploit the diversity of interests, needs, abilities, talents, and incomes of such populations by offering courses, workshops, institutes, and other such programs to those individuals, groups, and organizations that can afford to pay for largely fee-based programs. In these programs, which are focused largely on the intellectual growth and personal development needs and wants of targeted clientele, urban residents can find learning opportunities for just about any topic within the grasp of human imagination.

As urban areas continue to perceive the economic advantages of reducing housing segregation, and as people from diverse backgrounds continue to congregate in common spaces (such as schools, universities, and workplaces), individuals who grew up in segregated communities will be expected to interface effectively with individuals from other races, ethnicities, and cultures. There will therefore be increased need for the development of high-quality diversity training programs that can assist mainstreamed individuals and groups in urban areas to learn how to interact with and assist people from diverse cultural backgrounds in a culturally sensitive way. Such programs are especially important for administrators and professionals who are expected to lead a multicultural workforce. Without this preparation, the efforts of mainstreamed individuals working in racially and ethnically diverse environments are likely to fail. For example, Freeman, Brookhart, and Loadman (1999) studied the similarities and differences experienced by two groups of entry-level teachers from ten different teacher-preparation institutions: those who began their careers in racially and ethnically diverse schools (with 25 percent or more racial-minority students) and those who taught in schools with low levels of racial and ethnic diversity (with 10 percent or fewer racial-minority students). Although the two groups did not differ on most measures, beginning teachers in high-diversity schools did report lower levels of job satisfaction, greater difficulties in establishing meaningful relations with students, and higher levels of complexity in the teaching environment.

Programs Targeting Resource-Poor Communities. For the residents of communities such as Little Beirut who are without the income, prerequisite knowledge of the subject matter, transportation, child care, or other assets required to access and participate in those adult education program opportunities that are made available either in their communities or in the greater urban arena, the adult and continuing education system seems to have evolved a largely remedial effort that is funded primarily by third-party payers, such as the federal, state, or local government, philanthropic sources, churches, and other institutions. Such programs are often designed to address the most salient needs of inner-city residents. For example, the 1996 Personal Responsibility and Work Opportunity Act, the 1997 Welfare-to-Work program, and the Workforce Investment Act of 1998 (Hayes, 1999) included provisions that provided for the funding of mostly remedial adult education programs to address the remedial learning needs of unemployed and underemployed adults, many of whom reside in inner-city communities.

Amstutz and Sheared (2000), however, state that many of the educational programs that are intended to serve inner-city residents are failing miserably. They argue that the sociocultural, historical, and political marginalization of people of color, lower socioeconomic status workers, immigrants, the incarcerated, and the unemployed have often led to the development of programs that focus on redressing these individuals' deficits rather than on improving their strengths. Additionally, they observe, this marginalization is exacerbated by the fact that those who teach in many adult and vocational literacy programs are themselves marginalized due to their low salaries, lack of benefits, and temporary employment status.

To address more effectively the tremendous learning needs of inner-city communities, and to assist the entire urban community in participating in the global economy, adult educators should become more intricately involved in the federal, state, and metropolitan policy arenas where decisions are made regarding the allocation of scarce resources for the education of these adults. Once the programs are funded, they should provide a safe space for learning. Not only should the learning environment be free of physical violence, but it should also respect learners' initial language, culture, dress, celebrations, and styles of interacting while assisting them in learning new ways of viewing the world. The instructional staff and teachers should be informed and informative. These individuals should be not only competent in their subject matter areas, but also knowledgeable and understanding of the daily experiences and learning obstacles faced by inner-city residents. The curriculum and instructional approaches of these programs should integrate the lived experiences of students (via case studies, metaphors, similes, analogies, and so on) with instructional content and subject matter that address the learning needs of inner-city learners.

Conclusion

The urban context offers many challenges to adult educators seeking to deliver educational programs to the entire range of potential learners. There is a tremendous need for adult educators to take a proactive stance regarding the discriminatory practices that are endemic to urban areas. This will require the delivery of appropriate educational and training programs to mainstreamed individuals and communities on the sensitive topic of discriminatory behavior. For teaching those in resource-poor communities, the adult educator must rely on alternative funding sources to provide growth-oriented programs.

References

Abdul-Alim, J., and McBride, J. "Ten Held in Beating Death." *Milwaukee Journal Sentinel,* Oct. 2, 2002, pp. 1A, 14A.

Amstutz, D. D., and Sheared, V. "The Crisis in Adult Basic Education." *Education and Urban Society,* 2000, *32*(2), 155–166.

Barton, G. "Profiles: Crime, Gangs and Broken Homes Play a Large Part in Boys' Lives. *Milwaukee Journal Sentinel,* Oct. 3, 2002, pp. 1A, 16A.

Bender, T. "Urbanization." A&E Television Networks [http://historychannel.com/perl/print_book.pl?ID=35777], 2003.

Blakely, E. J. "A New Role for Education in Economic Development: Tomorrow's Economy Today." *Education and Urban Society,* 1997, *29*(4), 509–523.

Eyesberg, C. D. "The Origins of the American Urban System: Historical Accident and Initial Advantage." *Journal of Urban History,* 1989, *15*(2), 185–195.

Flowers, D. A. "Codeswitching and Ebonics in Urban Adult Basic Education Classrooms." *Education and Urban Society,* 2000, *32*(2), 221–236.

Freeman, D. J., Brookhart, S. M., and Loadman, W. E. "Realities of Teaching in Racially/Ethnically Diverse Schools: Feedback from Entry-Level Teachers. *Urban Education,* 1999, *34*(1), 89–114.

Galster, G. C., and Keeney, W. M. "Race, Residence, Discrimination, and Economic Opportunity: Modeling the Nexus of Urban Racial Phenomena." *Urban Affairs Quarterly,* 1988, *24*(1), 87–117.

Greer, S. "Urbanism and Urbanity: Cities in an Urban-Dominated Society." *Urban Affairs Quarterly,* 1989, *24*(3), 341–352.

Hacker, A. *Two Nations: Black and White, Separate, Hostile, Unequal.* New York: Ballantine, 1992.

Hayes, E. "Policy Issues That Drive the Transformation of Adult Literacy." In L. G. Martin and J. C. Fisher (eds.), *The Welfare-to-Work Challenge for Adult Literacy Educators.* New Directions for Adult and Continuing Education, no. 83. San Francisco: Jossey Bass, 1999.

Kasarda, J. D. "Urban Industrial Transition and the Underclass." *Annals of the American Academy of Political and Social Science,* 1989, *501,* 26–47.

McBride, J., and Ortiz, V. "Little Beirut: Violence, Anger Brewing in a Neighborhood That Is Poorer, Younger Than the Rest of the City." *Milwaukee Journal Sentinel,* Oct. 2, 2002, pp. 1A, 14A.

Quinn, L. M., and Pawasarat, J. *Racial Integration in Urban America: A Block Level Analysis of African American and White Housing Patterns.* Milwaukee, Wisc.: Employment and Training Institute, School of Continuing Education, University of Wisconsin-Milwaukee [http://www.uwm.edu/Dept/ETI/integration/integration.htm], 2003.

Rybarczyk, T. "Final Two Defendants Sentenced in Fatal Mob Beating." *Milwaukee Journal Sentinel,* July 22, 2003, pp. 1B–2B.

Turner, M. A., Ross, S., Galster, G., and Yingy, J. *Discrimination in Metropolitan Housing Markets: National Results from Phase I of HDS2000.* Washington, D.C.: U.S. Department of Housing and Urban Development [http://www.urban.org/urlprint.cfm?ID=8460], retrieved Nov. 7, 2002.

U.S. Census Bureau (2002). *Poverty in the United States: 2001—Current Population Reports: Consumer Income* [http://www.census.gov/prod/2002pubs/p60-219.pdf], retrieved Jan. 20, 2003.

Wilson, W. *The Truly Disadvantaged: The Inner City, the Underclass, and Public Policy.* Chicago: University of Chicago Press, 1987.

"Young Mother Awarded $1 Million." *Milwaukee Journal Sentinel,* July 1, 2003, pp. 1B–2B.

LARRY G. MARTIN is currently professor of adult and continuing education at the University of Wisconsin–Milwaukee.

2

To better understand the world of adult learners, we must remove ourselves from our ivory towers, classrooms, and offices and engage in the practice of adult education programs in urban settings.

Social and Cultural Issues in Urban Communities

Elice E. Rogers, Catherine A. Hansman

Adults face insurmountable change in the twenty-first century. These adjustments include shifting familial roles and responsibilities, continuing education due to changing workplace requirements, and living in an information age. The most sweeping change has been in the area of social policy, as evidenced by welfare reform legislation signed into law by President Clinton in 1996. Such legislation called for states to reduce their welfare rolls and restrict the time that families can receive welfare benefits (Waldron, Lavitt, and McConnaughy, 2001). Moreover, current policy changes in Temporary Aid to Needy Families (TANF) and the Work Investment Act permit the use of funds to assist low-income urban families and identify job retention and advancement as priorities (Martin and Fisher, 1999; Giloth and Gewirtz, 1999; Hayes, 1999).

As states have been successful in reducing the welfare rolls, welfare recipients and former welfare recipients have become increasingly concentrated in large urban areas. According to the U.S. Census Bureau (2002), the poverty rate in the United States rose to 11.7 percent in 2001, while the median household income declined 2.2 percent. In real terms, this translates to 32.9 million people living in poverty. Poor families increased from 6.4 million in 2000 to 6.8 million in 2002. Increases in poverty were concentrated in cities, where 16.5 percent of the population is considered poor. Additionally, many of the low-income and urban poor are women, people of color, and immigrants (Freedman, Gennetian, Knab, and Navarro, 2000; Illinois Refugee Social Services Consortium and Women's Bureau, n.d.). Forty-six percent of female-headed households with children less than eighteen years old are below the poverty line (Sheared, McCabe, and Umeki,

NEW DIRECTIONS FOR ADULT AND CONTINUING EDUCATION, no. 101, Spring 2004 © Wiley Periodicals, Inc.

2000). Further, more than 55 percent of female-headed households maintained by African American and Latina American women are poor (Bing and Trotman Reid, 1996). Sociologists such as William Julius Wilson (1987) maintain that the socioeconomic conditions of many urban cities have been transformed such that neighborhoods are populated by the most economically disadvantaged individuals, who lack training, and that their families experience long spells of poverty and being on welfare.

It is our contention that, as Cervero, Wilson, and Associates (2001, p. 2) say, "adult education cannot be a neutral activity in the continual struggle for the distribution of knowledge and power in society." To better assist adult learners in the urban context, educators must attend to two things. First, we must adhere to Lindeman's (1926) call to help adults process education, acquire the necessary tools (that is, information, new knowledge, and training), and adapt to the changing world around them, because "changed individuals will have the collective effect of changing society" (Merriam and Brockett, 1997, p. 91). Second, we have the responsibility to integrate urban issues into adult education by returning to practice (Daley, Fisher, and Martin, 2000). In other words, to better understand the world of adult learners, we must remove ourselves from our ivory towers, classrooms, and offices and engage in the practice of adult education programs in urban settings. For it is in practice, in community, and in the social context that we acknowledge the urban community, and the urban adult as a diverse source of knowledge (Hamilton and Cunningham, 1989).

This chapter explicates the problems that adult education practitioners confront in assisting residents of low-income urban communities to access and utilize educational opportunities. Our preliminary discussion is informed by an analysis of the contemporary literature on welfare-to-work, family literacy, adult literacy, job training, federal legislation, government reports, adult education agencies, programs servicing low-income urban adult participants, and workforce development initiatives focused on disadvantaged urban adults. Three problems faced by adult education practitioners emerge from the literature: confronting a crisis in literacy, addressing the needs of low-income urban participants, and working in the face of policy. We first discuss these problems, then we integrate urban issues by returning to practice and examining three organizations in the Greater Cleveland Area that serve low-income urban adults and describe how they provide educational services. We close with discussion of implications for adult education practitioners and academicians.

A Crisis in Literacy: An Ideological Dilemma

Many adults who come to adult education programs are treated as objects rather than as subjects and thus their knowledge and experience in terms of how they see and view the world are rendered invisible. Moreover, the emphasis in many adult education programs is on providing participants with the kind of capital that will enable them to be successful in American society (Sheared, McCabe, and Umeki, 2000). According to the functional literacy paradigm, the appropriate capital can be cultivated by focusing on participants' ability to read, write, and interpret; cultural literacy, on the other hand, posits that the ideal cultural capital can be obtained through learning, mastering, and articulating cultural content that reflects the dominant culture (Amstutz and Sheared, 2000).

Lack of consideration for adult learners adds to their lack of privilege in formal educational settings, resulting in institutions practicing the "politics of neglect" (Sissel, Hansman, and Kasworm, 2001, p. 17). The politics of neglect may help to explain why urban adults choose to participate or not participate in an adult education program. The politics of neglect are further evidenced in a study of reasons that Chicano and Chicana adults do not participate in adult basic education (Sparks, 1994). Sparks describes the participants in these programs as exhibiting a "tremendous cultural pride and identity which influences individual decisions and actions to engage in culturally insensitive social institutions; a majority of individuals report past efforts to upgrade academic and vocational skills; and almost all study participants indicated a lack of faith in the dominant enterprise of education based on experiences of educational exclusion (youth and/or adult), intercultural struggles, and larger social and economic inequalities" (p. 4). Clearly, as indicated in Spark's study, the culture and needs of adult learners are routinely discounted by educators when planning programs for adult learners.

Many educators of adults find themselves in literacy dilemmas as they are challenged to move low-income urban adults to self-sufficiency, all the while operating under an umbrella of structural constraints and in a system that views low-income adults as problem people who are the "sore thumbs" of society (Askov, 2000; Amstutz and Sheared, 2000). As a result, participants' needs are avoided, neglected, and overlooked, and their needs are negotiated without consulting them. Amstutz and Sheared (2000) advocate critical literacy as a paradigm for practitioners of adult education to address urban participants' real needs. Critical literacy views adult participants as subjects rather than as objects. It recognizes participants' voices as their own racial, gendered being operating in many contexts, which influences how they view the world. Practitioners embracing critical literacy have assessed their own position and power and work to encourage adults to utilize their own knowledge in assessing their circumstances in ways that will work not only to improve their lives but also to manage and control their urban communities (Amstutz and Sheared, 2000; Sparks and Peterson, 2000).

The City Mission of Cleveland, Ohio, which has a ninety-year history, is an example of a multifaceted adult education provider that views the adult participant as subject rather than object. It reaches out to thousands of people in the Cleveland area by extending a helping hand. The City Mission of Cleveland strives to provide food, clothing, and shelter for the homeless, as well as health care for the sick. In addressing the varying needs of diverse adults, the City Mission values urban adult participants as diverse persons possessing dignity and worth (see http://www.thecitymission.org).

Addressing the Needs of Low-Income Urban Participants

Practitioners of urban adult education also face a formidable challenge in working with the varied needs of participants. The participants in an adult education program for low-income urban adults must assess their time in view of the competing demands imposed on them in other areas of their lives. Lack of money, inability to care for children and other family members, transportation problems, and lack of time have been identified as reasons that urban adults do not participate in adult education programs (Waldron, Lavitt, and McConnaughy, 2001; Coyle, Williams, and Taylor, 1973). Just arranging for the care of children or other family members, or for transportation to and from the adult education program, may be arduous given limited financial resources.

The causes of poverty and homelessness are embedded in a complex web of economic and social structures within the United States. Moreover, insidious social practices blame the victims themselves for their circumstances—a game that is devastating to those in precarious positions. As Clarke and others (1996, p. 54) describe, "Education in life skills and job training that might prevent homelessness are unavailable to those who most need them. Services to materially poor people in general and homeless people in particular are delivered in a punative and miserly way... Solutions to homelessness are seen in purely physical and quantitative terms, not in terms of human and community development."

There are no easy fixes for the situations in which low-income urban adults find themselves, so the question is, Where can they turn for assistance? And assuming that there are helpful agencies that can aid them, what is the role of adult education in their lives, or in the lives of other adults in urban settings? Wilson and Hayes (2000, p. 17) contend that "adult and continuing education is... a social practice of human interaction that depends significantly upon its practitioners' assumptions, values, and experiences to shape practical actions, actions... that are profoundly affected by the larger socio-cultural-economic-political conditions in which they take place." The urban setting provides a unique set of issues in a complicated sociopolitical arena that frames adult education practice and challenges educators of urban adults.

In addition to the aforementioned problems, urban low-income adults may need assistance and support with English in programs that acknowledge their multifaceted, diverse identities (race, class, gender, and language). Urban adult education programs that fail to recognize the multiple literacies that emerge as a result of participants' multifaceted identities are sending a strong message to participants that English literacy is the only literacy that matters (Sparks, 1994). Also, among low-income urban residents, practitioners of adult education will encounter participants who are in need of counseling or other support mechanisms to assist them in dealing with personal, health, and legal problems directly related to housing accommodations, drug abuse, domestic violence, disabilities (visible and invisible), criminal behavior, and violations of the law that may lead to incarceration or parole (Hayes, 1999; Brown, 2000; Waldron, Lavitt, and McConnaughy, 2001). In response to these varying issues, Fisher (1999) argues that the practitioners who run adult education programs must rethink the needs of urban adult participants and begin to reconceptualize their programs and their roles as urban practitioners to address these needs.

We found that the Empowerment Center of Greater Cleveland (ECGC), established in 1966 as a grassroots movement serving low-income people of diverse ethnic backgrounds, is an example of an adult education provider that addresses the diverse needs of its participants, as evidenced through its programming (Empowerment Center of Greater Cleveland, 2003a, 2003b). Programs offered by the Empowerment Center include a family services center that aids families in accessing community services. The ECGC also provides direct networks to budget counseling, food, health care, child care, emotional support counseling, legal assistance, shelter, and tax assistance and preparation.

Policy Matters

At the heart of policy matters lies a struggle for knowledge and power. Urban adult practitioners across the United States are extremely frustrated with local, state, and federal policy and with how it affects the access of residents of low-income communities to educational opportunities. The following five concerns raised by the literature are overwhelming and perplexing policy challenges:

1. *Inadequate, unclear, and uncoordinated policies.* Some states are taking action to move low-income urban adults out of poverty; however, such efforts are at best unclear and unrelated to the varying approaches used to assist low-income and poor adults. Moreover, local, state and federal policies do not represent one universal package of applicability for practitioners. At each level there are guidelines and policies that specify the conditions required for education and training (Clymer, Roberts, and Strawn, 2001).

2. *Poor understanding of urban low-income adults.* Policies directly tied to education and training are many times constructed in ways that do not directly address or consider the specific needs of the low-income urban adult population. Policy expectations rarely take into account the voice, reality, problems, and lives of the participants. New policies might consider, for instance, integrating adult education with activities for participants' children, because as the lives of individuals improve, so do the lives

of their families (Greenberg and Strawn, 1991; Hayes, 1999; Sparks and Peterson, 2000).

3. *Little emphasis on combining continuing supportive education with work.* In many instances, policies dictate that urban low-income adults must receive training or basic education as a prerequisite to employment, but little education or training after they are employed. As low income adults move toward economic self-sufficiency, policies should support continual education, because credentials appear to be a factor in helping adults attain upward mobility (Greenberg and Strawn, 1991; Hayes, 1999).

4. *No recognition of the marginalization of urban adult education programs and providers.* Many urban practitioners describe policies that require them to do more to assist urban residents with increasingly minimal resources. Practitioners also report that they work in urban programs that are underfunded, and that they rely on part-time personnel, thus contributing to their own marginalization (Sheared, McCabe, and Umeki, 2000, Amstutz and Sheared, 2000; Sparks and Peterson, 2000).

5. *Tension in accountability.* The issue of accountability for urban practitioners looks in large part at meeting and serving the expectations of many interests, which can prove challenging. These multiple interests include the funder, the provider or program, the urban practitioners, and the low-income urban participants. Urban practitioners are continually operating under pressure to respond to these varying and competing interests (Sparks and Peterson, 2000; Cervero, Wilson, and Associates, 1994).

Given that these issues raise more questions than answers, what can urban practitioners do in light of these policy inconsistencies and problems? How can urban practitioners work to ensure that the needs of low-income urban adult learners are met in the midst of bureaucracy, politics, procedures, processes, and protocol? Most important, how can urban practitioners be assured that policy matters do not inhibit but rather expand access and promote opportunity for low-income urban residents?

To begin to understand who benefits, whose interests are legitimately served, and how politics and power are constituted in policy matters, urban adult education practitioners must become knowledgeable about legislation affecting adult learners and low-income adults on the local, state, and national levels. Further, these practitioners should be involved in formulating and constructing matters of policy. Finally, by being active in policy initiatives, urban practitioners can network with one another while collectively addressing what does not work, seeking corrections, and arguing for improvements in policies (Cervero, Wilson, and Associates, 2001; Hansman, 2001; Hayes, 1999). We found the ECGC to be a notable example of an adult education provider that is active in policy initiatives and in understanding how such initiatives affect its clientele. Inherent in the mission of the ECGC is that changes in social welfare policy are made with the input of urban participants (Empowerment Center of Greater Cleveland, 2003a, 2003b).

Thus far we have examined the sociocultural literature, explicating the problems and issues that urban adult education practitioners confront in assisting residents of low-income urban communities to access educational opportunities. We now integrate urban issues by exploring examples of practice in various urban programs in the greater Cleveland, Ohio, area, looking specifically at the Escuela Popular, Hard Hatted Women, and the Council for Economic Opportunities in Greater Cleveland. These three organizations serve low-income urban residents.

Escuela Popular

Escuela Popular, a community-based organization, has been operating in the Tremont area of Cleveland for the past ten years. Escuela Popular emphasizes the culture of the community and the role of both student and practitioner as co-learners in fostering social change. All participants focus on language and culture. Escuela Popular has a unique and rather innovative English as a Second Language (ESL) for Survival Program (see http://povertycenter.cwru.edu/west%20Resource%inventory.htm).

The ESL program includes courses in language, computers, and cultural arts. In the language courses, urban adult participants receive free English instruction. These courses generally meet once a week, are taught by volunteers, and have a student body of primarily non-English speakers and speakers of English who are working to enhance their reading, writing, and English comprehension skills. Computer courses are taught in Spanish over a ten-week period at a cost of twenty-five dollars. In this small-group course, urban adults learn how to repair computers by completing rehabilitation projects. After completing the projects, these participants, who are working to improve their computer literacy skills, are allowed to keep the computers they have repaired. Cultural arts courses include Latin dance and Afro-Caribbean drumming; they emphasize Latino and other cultures in the Greater Cleveland area. In addition to these courses, the ESL program supports and endorses work skills training, community skills training, and community activist training. A majority of the Escuela Popular practitioners are noncertified teachers, representing women and people of color. The instructional strategies that these practitioners employ are not always indicative of those found in formal educational settings, and graduates of the program do not receive an official diploma, degree, or certificate.

Hard Hatted Women

Founded in 1979 as a support group for women and incorporated as a non-profit organization in the state of Ohio, Hard Hatted Women (HHW) is committed to encouraging and empowering women in the Greater Cleveland area toward self-sufficiency by emphasizing and promoting work in the technical and training areas. Urban adult residents representing primarily low-income households receive training, support services, and placement assistance. HHW has cultivated partnerships that are essential to the economic and workforce development policy and initiatives of the Greater Cleveland area. It is through these partnering relationships that HHW is able to generate and provide technical assistance to more than one hundred and fifty unions and corporations, with a special focus on the industrial areas.

Jobs in the skilled trades can move low-income urban women out of their current condition because these jobs offer wide-ranging benefits, including comprehensive health care plans that are crucial to the overall well-being of families. Following a three- or four-week period of training, depending on the trade, women can earn up to $28 per hour. The organization operates with a six-person staff. Funding and support come from government, corporate, and foundation grants, corporate and individual donations, fees for service, and membership dues.

HHW has three central educational features. The first is *career training and development,* administered via a pre-apprenticeship training (PAT) program. The PAT program runs ten weeks; its curriculum emphasizes job training and education. The program is the mechanism that prepares women for and orients them to the barriers they will face as women working in traditionally male-dominated, blue-collar professions. The PAT program also provides proficiency testing, counseling, math tutoring, resume techniques, and all the services vital to assisting urban adult women in securing and maintaining good positions in the skilled and technical professions.

The second component of HHW is *leadership development.* Graduates of HHW as well as HHW board members collaborate to create opportunities for current program participants. Service is also tied to HHW's third and last component: *supportive services, training, and community outreach.* Over the years HHW has established a reputation of placing women in trades and skilled positions, and this reputation has led employers, unions, and others within the city of Cleveland to seek out its services. Further, community-driven initiatives mandate the hiring of women and people of color; HHW helps to turn these mandates into reality. HHW recently received its second Women in Apprenticeship and Non-Traditional Occupations grant from the U.S. Department of Labor's Women's Bureau. More than 359 women have graduated from the PAT program; 226 women have obtained jobs, making an average of $11.40 per hour, and 57 percent of the 226 have secured union jobs (*Hard Hatted Women Pre-Apprentice Training Program,* 2000; http://www.hardhattedwomen.org/Career.htm).

Council for Economic Opportunities in Greater Cleveland

The Council for Economic Opportunities in Greater Cleveland (CEOGC) was established under the Economic Opportunities Act of 1964. The CEOGC has administered antipoverty and empowerment programs to the residents of Greater Cleveland for more than thirty-five years. Its mission is to promote economic self-sufficiency for low-income families and individuals through career training and entry into the job market (http://www.ceogc.org).

The CGOEC offers programs in General Educational Development (GED), Customer Service and Relations (CSR), Office Management Technologies, English as a Second Language (ESL), and Workforce Development. The goal of these programs is to help participants gain needed skills. For example, the CSR program is for high school or GED graduates and provides training in the fast-growing customer service representative field. The ESL program lasts sixteen weeks and is designed to give low-income and unemployed non-English-speaking newcomers to urban America an opportunity to learn basic language and cultural skills for functioning in American society. The Workforce Development program provides individual counseling, training in workplace skills, and job placement services. Instructors work one-on-one with participants to coach them. The CEOGC also supports all of the Head Start programs in Greater Cleveland.

Discussion and Implications for Practice

The organizations described in this chapter are similar to other urban organizations across the United States in their provision of assistance to adults. What is unique, however, in how they address the role of adult education in facilitating personal and social transformation for low-income urban adults is that they provide educational opportunities that can assist urban participants in the programs. These organizations effectively provide these opportunities because embedded in their *how* is a staged "retreat to the margins" (West, 1992, p. 46)—to the urban poor, the low-income, the disenfranchised, the disadvantaged, the marginalized, and the oppressed (Hull, 1992). By retreating to the margins, adult education programs more fully serve the diverse needs of their participants while encouraging the development of reflective practitioners to facilitate these programs.

Reflective practitioners of urban adult education recognize that the intentions of legislation, adult basic education, adult literacy, job training, and welfare-to-work programs do not always match the reality of the lives of the participants at the margins, or the type of support available for programs to serve urban adults. The literature and cases discussed in this chapter suggest that to facilitate personal and social transformation among adult learners and urban low-income adults, reflective practitioners must examine the margins for effective and just practice. Reflective practitioners understand that the application of instructional strategies, lesson plans, curriculum models, training modules, competency-based assessments, and subsistence work by educators of urban adults is meaningless to the urban poor if these tools do not change their circumstances or improve their economic conditions.

We further argue that personal and social transformation in the lives of the urban poor and low-income residents is not possible without economic transformation. Providing education and training but not work does not permit economic freedom and limits urban adult participation as well as the acquisition of knowledge and power. Reflective practitioners of urban adult education do not believe that adult education is a neutral activity in the continual struggle for the distribution of knowledge and power in society (Cervero, Wilson, and Associates, 2001). Rather, adult education practitioners need to recognize this struggle and begin to frame and plan programs with and for their participants by keeping in mind the respective needs of people at the margins. We believe that it is our responsibility as adult education practitioners to respond to the needs of the urban community. Finally, it is our duty as adult education academicians to promote social responsibility in our students in order to "enhance the quality of human life in all its personal and social dimensions" (Merriam and Brockett, 1997, p. 82).

References

Amstutz, D. D., and Sheared, V. "The Crisis in Adult Basic Education." *Education and Urban Society,* 2000, *32*(2), 155–166.

Askov, E. N. "Adult Literacy." In A. Wilson and E. Hayes (eds.), *Handbook of Adult and Continuing Education.* San Francisco: Jossey-Bass, 2000.

Bing, V. M., and Trotman Reid, P. "Unknown Women and Unknowing Research." In N. Goldberger, J. Tarule, B. Clinchy, and M. Belenky (eds.), *Knowledge, Difference and Power.* New York: Basic Books, 1996.

Brown, R. "Helping Low-Income Mothers with Criminal Records Achieve Self-Sufficiency. *Welfare Information Network Issue Notes,* 2000, *4*(13), 2–9 [http://www.welfareinfo.org/lowincomemothersissuenote.htm].

Cervero, R. M., Wilson, A. L., and Associates. *Planning Responsibly for Adult Education: A Guide to Negotiating Power and Interests.* San Francisco: Jossey-Bass, 1994.

Cervero, R. M., Wilson, A. L., and Associates. "At the Heart of Practice: The Struggle for Knowledge and Power." In R. Cervero and A. Wilson (eds.), *Power in Practice: Adult Education and the Struggle for Knowledge and Power in Society.* San Francisco: Jossey-Bass, 2001.

Clarke, D., Dell, D., Farrell, B., Gray, D., Santiago, B., Utley, T., and Kennedy, M. "A Hole in My Soul: The Experiences of Homeless Women." In D. Dujon and A. Withorn (eds.), *For Crying Out Loud: Women's Poverty in the United States.* Boston: South End Press, 1996.

Clymer, C., Roberts, B., and Strawn, J. *States of Change: Policies and Programs to Promote Low-Wage Workers' Steady Employment and Advancement* (CE 081 885). Field Report Series. Philadelphia: Public/Private Ventures, May 2001. (ED 454 387).

Coyle, H. F., Williams, G., and Taylor, M. (1973). *Project Total—To Teach All: An Inquiry into the Development of a Model for Identifying Unmet Needs in Urban Postsecondary Educational Offerings—Final Report* (CE 001 521). Akron, Ohio: Center for Urban Studies, 1973. (ED 092 779).

Daley, B. J., Fisher, J. C., and Martin, L. G. "Urban Contexts for Adult Education Practice." In A. Wilson and E. Hayes (eds.), *Handbook of Adult and Continuing Education.* San Francisco: Jossey-Bass, 2000.

Empowerment Center of Greater Cleveland. *Public Education and Awareness Department.* Cleveland, Ohio: Empowerment Center of Greater Cleveland, 2003a. Brochure.

Empowerment Center of Greater Cleveland. Brochure. Cleveland, Ohio: Empowerment Center of Greater Cleveland, 2003b.

Fisher, J. C. "Research on Adult Literacy Education in the Welfare-to-Work Transition." In L. Martin and J. Fisher (eds.), *The Welfare-to-Work Challenge for Adult Literacy Educators*. New Directions For Adult and Continuing Education, no. 83. San Francisco: Jossey-Bass, 1999.

Freedman, S., Gennetian, L.A., Knab, J., and Navarro, D. *The Los Angeles Jobs-First GAIN Evaluation: Final Report on a Work First Program in a Major Urban Center*. New York: Manpower Demonstration Research Corporation [http://www.mdrc.org/publications/37/execsum.html], June 2000.

Giloth, B., and Gewirtz, S. *Retaining Low-Income Residents in the Workforce: Lessons from the Annie Casey Jobs Initiative* (CE 083 310). St. Paul, Minn.: Annie Casey Foundation, 1999. (ED 346 082).

Greenberg, M., and Strawn, J. JOBS in the South: The Impact of Low Welfare Benefits and Low Education Levels (CE 058665). Washington, D.C.: Center for Law and Social Policy, 1991. (ED 335 502).

Hamilton, E., and Cunningham, P. M. "Community-Based Adult Education." In S. Merriam and P. Cunningham (eds.), *Handbook of Adult and Continuing Education*. San Francisco: Jossey-Bass, 1989.

Hansman, C. A. "The Political Landscape of Adult Education: From the Personal to the Political and Back Again." In C. Hansman and P. Sissel (eds.), *The Political Landscape of Adult Education*. New Directions for Adult and Continuing Education, no. 91. San Francisco: Jossey-Bass, 2001.

Hard Hatted Women Pre-Apprentice Training Program. Cleveland, Ohio: Hard Hatted Women, 2000. Brochure.

Hayes, E. "Policy Issues That Drive the Transformation of Adult Literacy." In L. Martin and J. Fisher (eds.), *Policy Issues That Drive the Transformation of Adult Literacy*. New Directions for Adult and Continuing Education, no. 83. San Francisco: Jossey-Bass, 1999.

Hull, G. *Their Chances? Slim and None: An Ethnographic Account of the Experiences of Low-Income People of Color in a Vocational Program at Work*(CE 062418). Berkeley: National Center for Research in Vocational Education, University of California, 1992. (ED 351 553).

Lindeman, E. *The Meaning of Adult Education*. Norman: University of Oklahoma, 1949. (Originally published 1926.)

Martin, L. G., and Fisher, J. C. "Editors' Notes." In L. G. Martin and J. C. Fisher (eds.), *The Welfare-to-Work Challenge for Adult Literacy Educators*. New Directions for Adult and Continuing Education, no. 83. San Francisco: Jossey-Bass, 1999.

Merriam, S. B., and Brockett, R. G. *The Profession and Practice of Adult Education*. San Francisco: Jossey-Bass, 1997.

Illinois Refugee Social Services Consortium and Women's Bureau, Region V, U.S. Department of Labor. *Moving from Welfare to Work: The Experiences of Refugee Women in Illinois*. Washington, D.C.: U.S. Department of Labor, Women's Bureau [www.dol.gov/wb/info_about_wb/regions/refugee.pdf], n.d.

Sheared, V., McCabe, J., and Umeki, D. "Adult Literacy and Welfare Reform Marginalization, Voice, and Control." *Education and Urban Society*, 2000, 32(2), 167–187.

Sissel, P. A., Hansman, C. A., and Kasworm, C. E. "The Politics of Neglect: Adult Learners in Higher Education." In C. Hansman and P. Sissel (eds.), *The Political Landscape of Adult Education*. New Directions for Adult and Continuing Education, no. 91. San Francisco: Jossey-Bass, 2001.

Sparks, B. *Structural-Cultural Factors of Nonparticipation in Adult Basic Education by Chicano/a Adults in Urban Communities in Colorado*. Final Section 353 Project Report (CE 70673). Denver: Colorado State Department of Education. Washington, D.C.: U.S. Department of Education, Office of Vocational and Adult Education, 1994.

Sparks, B., and Peterson, E. A. "Adult Basic Education and the Crisis of Accountability." In A. Wilson and E. Hayes (eds.), *Handbook of Adult and Continuing Education*. San Francisco: Jossey-Bass, 2000.

U.S. Census Bureau. *Poverty in the United States: 2001*. [http://www.census.gov/hhes/www/poverty01.html], retrieved Dec. 11, 2002.

Waldron, V. R., Lavitt, L., and McConnaughy, M. "Welfare-to-Work: An Analysis of the Communication Competencies Taught in a Job Training Program Serving an Urban Poverty Area." *Communication Education*, 2001, *50*, 15–33.

West, L. *A View from the Margins: Access to Higher Education for Adults in Inner-City America*. Open Seminar Series, occasional paper 1, Unit for the Study of Continuing Education (CE 063476). Canterbury, England: University of Kent, 1992. (ED 356 385).

Wilson, A. L., and Hayes. E. R. "On Thought and Action in Adult and Continuing Education." In A. Wilson and E. Hayes (eds.), *Handbook of Adult and Continuing Education*. San Francisco: Jossey-Bass, 2000.

Wilson, W. J. *The Truly Disadvantaged: The Inner City, the Underclass, and Public Policy*. Chicago: University of Chicago Press, 1987.

ELICE E. ROGERS is assistant professor of adult learning and development at Cleveland State University.

CATHERINE A. HANSMAN is associate professor and director of graduate programs in adult learning and development at Cleveland State University.

3

Educators of urban adults should attempt to deconstruct the dynamics in the classroom that replicate the social, political, and economic discourse of the dominant group. We must work to surface the complexity of diverse experiences represented by multiple oppressed groups.

Discriminative Justice: Can Discrimination Be Just?

Tonette S. Rocco, Suzanne J. Gallagher

This chapter examines the nature and importance of discriminative justice in urban adult and higher education. Adult education practitioners often receive conflicting messages from the literature and legal sources regarding the appropriateness of discriminating against or discriminating in favor of certain categories of people on the grounds of ethnicity or gender (Bagnall, 1995) or other determinants of privilege (Rocco and West, 1998). Discrimination for or against particular people then becomes a matter of who participates, who completes, and who benefits—What then becomes the classroom and program dynamics of our urban educational centers?

In an attempt to enhance the discourse on discriminatory justice begun by Bagnall (1995), we discuss justice, oppression, power, and privilege. Critical race theory (Bell, 1992; Delgado and Stefanic, 2001; Freeman, 1995; Ladson-Billings, 2000) provides the legal analysis of discrimination that we use to assist educators of adults in constructing knowledge about privilege, oppression, and justice in urban adult education. The chapter is divided into four main sections that discuss, respectively, discriminative justice, discrimination, antidiscrimination law, and implications for adult and higher education.

Discriminative Justice

Discrimination is "the denial of institutional access on the basis of ethnic or racial identity" (Cornell and Hartmann, 1998, p. 169). While *Webster's New Explorer Dictionary and Thesaurus* (1999, p. 149) defines discrimination as to "distinguish, differentiate" or "to make a difference in treatment on a

NEW DIRECTIONS FOR ADULT AND CONTINUING EDUCATION, no. 101, Spring 2004 © Wiley Periodicals, Inc.

basis other than individual merit," noticeably absent from the dictionary definition is a specific reference to group identity, which broadens the scope beyond the traditional discourse on race, ethnicity, and gender. Discrimination acts as a boundary mechanism that denies access to employment, education and political, civic, and social opportunities. Discrimination is considered by civil rights proponents (Peterson, 1999) to be behavior that can be outlawed.

Discriminative justice is an elusive term being used only by Bagnall (1995), who situates his discussion of discrimination in a postmodern framework. Postmodernity "incorporates but problematizes modernity," which is the quest for "universal foundations of truth, morality, and aesthetics, in the pursuit of human emancipation" (p. 81). Problematizing modernity generates a plurality of possible beliefs, meanings, actions, and power where there is or can be no one right set of beliefs. For Bagnall, "The state is therefore denied any a priori substantive grounds for privileging one set of beliefs over others" (p. 82).

Bagnall shows the untenable distinction between two forms of discrimination, including discriminative perception and discriminative action. *Discriminative perception* is the recognition of differences between individuals and things. The perceived differences are influenced by the expectations, values, and beliefs we bring to the situation. Perception is influenced by the present perceived difference between the individuals or things and "by the experience of past actions and the anticipation of future ones" (p. 84). *Discriminative action* is "that which is done in response to the recognition of difference" (p. 83). Discriminative action is both based on and constrained by an individual's set of beliefs and values.

The occurrences of perception and action are not separate; rather, perception is embedded in the discourse of discriminative action. This means that the expectations, norms, and values we bring to the situation shape the perception of difference and are outcomes of the prior evaluation of difference. For example, if I grew up in a community that condemned homosexuality as a sin, my perception of gay men and lesbians will be evaluated in light of this particular discourse. If I grew up in a community that embraced a continuum of sexual orientations as natural biological occurrences, I would not perceive gay, lesbian, and bisexual people as abnormal or deviant. On the basis of these perceptions, the actions taken by those who condemn homosexuality can be deadly for members of the group condemned, as in the Mathew Shepard case (Swigonski, Mama, and Ward, 2001), and a reason for migration to urban centers; and the actions taken by those who embrace a continuum of sexual orientations tend to be life affirming, as in the case of legally and socially sanctioned adoptions by gay and lesbian people.

While Bagnall's postmodern framework of discriminative justice of perception and action is helpful, it does not expose the contextualized dynamics of injustice, oppression, privilege, and power that support the system of discrimination. He does not specifically define justice; he identifies it as the negotiation of different discourses. He indicates that discriminative judgments are "grounded in and negotiated between particular discourses" (1995, p. 88) and that these judgments are partial. In fact, Bagnall (1995, p. 88) contends that "beyond the level of private understanding, discrimination, in itself, is neither conservative nor reformist, neither just nor unjust." Discriminative action may be unjust when it ignores perceived injustice from past actions and allows tolerance to become so broad that it becomes indifferent. Bagnall quotes Bauman (1991), who says that postmodernism values tolerance, allowing us to have an "attitude of indifference-fed callousness" to suffering (p. 9). While using discriminative criteria to take action on behalf of or against an individual is just, discrimination becomes unjust when action is taken because the individual is a member of a group (Bagnall, 1995).

Past actions are captured in processes and patterns of justice or injustice. Knowledge, meaning, and belief are trapped in the linguistic and perceptual frameworks that emerge from specific social and political systems. These systems require an enhanced discourse of justice and oppression, power and privilege, to deconstruct and contextualize Bagnall's notion of discriminative justice.

Toward an Understanding of Discrimination

To understand discrimination, we must understand the contextualized dynamics that support the capability to discriminate. These dynamics are controlled by the dominant group in a society. We here discuss justice, oppression, power, and privilege in an effort to understand the forces underlying discrimination.

Justice. Sen's (1999) perspective on justice is derived from the utilitarian and libertarian perspectives, which value certain bases of information, including the outcomes that people have reason to value (that is, income, liberties, happiness, and so on). The capability approach to justice evaluates it in terms of the freedom people have to take action and choose lives they value (Sen, 1999). For instance, Sen (1999, p. 75) writes, "The evaluative focus of this 'capability approach' can be either on the realized functionings (what a person is actually able to do) or on the capability set of alternatives she has (her real opportunities)."

The capability approach examines the relationship between a person's functioning set and his or her capability set. The *functioning set* contains the outcomes or things a person may value being or doing (Sen, 1999). The *capability set* is the functioning set that is realistic for a person to achieve (Sen, 1999). The functioning set for a middle-class mother and that for a poor mother to attend adult education classes are the same. The capability set for each is markedly different from that of the other. The poor mother is less likely to have access to transportation and child care, which can affect class attendance. The middle-class mother has more resources to draw from, such as discretionary income and time. The capability set reveals the freedom or lack of freedom to achieve valued outcomes. The poor mother's choice to attend adult education classes is limited by a diminished capability set, based in oppressive or discriminatory economic and political systems. (See the case of Little Beirut in Martin, Chapter One, this volume, for a good example of oppressive economic and political systems that limit people's capability sets.)

The capability approach uses information about peoples' ability to choose lives they value as the measure of justice (Sen, 1999). This measure of justice is not "all or none" but reflects the heterogeneous outcomes that people value. For example, people may exercise their right to migrate to urban communities for economic opportunity, but if the air in these communities is contaminated by incinerators burning garbage, their capability to enjoy a good quality of life is diminished. What is not immediately evident in this information is that people are not free to choose to move from these urban environments or to get better health care. By viewing this information through the capability approach, the lack of freedom to make other choices is revealed. Injustice is measured not only by the levels of poverty or patterns of disease but also by diminished freedom to act and choose. The solutions for fixing injustice do not stop at providing material support but require the development of capacity and the freedom to make choices.

Oppression. Understanding the processes of oppression offers the possibility to act discriminatively to change unjust systems. Oppression is "systematic institutional processes which prevent some people from learning and using satisfying and expansive skills in socially recognized settings, or institutionalized social processes which inhibit people's ability to play and communicate with others or to express their feelings and perspectives on social life where others can listen" (Young, 1990, p. 38). Oppression consists of processes that result in the replication of injustice in society: marginalization, powerlessness, cultural imperialism, systematic violence, and exploitation against the social group (Young, 1990).

Marginalization is the process of excluding people from centers of power and influence, such as the system of labor (Young, 1990). This process is begun early by tying the educational system to workforce education. Marginalization begins by manifesting itself throughout the life cycle of education and labor by socializing people for different occupations that determine lifestyle choices and socioeconomic status (Eckert, 1989). This preparation also influences who takes part in urban adult education programs. For instance, people of lower socioeconomic status and racially marked individuals are more likely to participate in government-run remedial programs, while individuals of higher socioeconomic status who lack race consciousness generally have employers who encourage and supplement their higher educational pursuits.

People who are racially marked—blacks and Native Americans, old people, mentally and physically disabled people, and other people who are involuntarily unemployed or underemployed, lack access to urban adult education programs, or are silenced in our classrooms—are examples of marginalized groups. Social welfare mitigates the group's circumstances but does not allow marginalized people to exercise their capabilities and their freedom to choose. Marginalization of oppressed groups diminishes their opportunity for self-development and perpetuates patterns of distributive injustice.

Powerlessness is evident in workplaces and urban education centers where employees and students have little or no say in policy decisions that affect them directly. "Most workplaces are not organized democratically, direct participation in public policy decisions is rare, and policy implementation is for the most part hierarchical, imposing rules on bureaucrats and citizens" (Young, 1990, p. 56). Nonprofessionals do not participate in decisions that affect their lives and the conditions of their employment and are rarely listened to in the decision-making process.

Cultural imperialism involves two primary dynamics. The first dynamic is the dominant group's ability to "render the particular perspective of one's own group invisible" (Young, pp. 58–59), making the dominant group's power implicit and assumed. At the same time, the second dynamic of cultural imperialism stereotypes the dominated group and labels it the "other" (Goffman, 1963). Oppression does not allow for a positive appreciation of group difference. Thus, dominated groups and group members experience the oppression of invisibility and stereotyping, leading to high incidences of alcoholism, drug use, depression, and so on (Pharr, 1988). Oppression maintains a political system in which those in power create adult education programs believing that *they know* what is best for learners, thus denying learners a voice in the planning process (Cervero and Wilson, 2001; Sheared, 1999).

As Young (1990, p. 62) writes, "violence is systemic because it is directed at members of a group simply because they are members of that group." The layers of systemic violence include acts of violence, threats of violence, and lack of punishment for violence. Systemic violence limits self-development in members of oppressed groups. It is evidenced when students fear going to specific venues on campus or revealing their experience in the classroom. Living with the threat of violence deprives targeted group members of energy and the freedom to act. For instance, a black man entering a library late at night uses energy worrying about the potential negative reactions of white female patrons, and a lesbian woman entering a library late at night uses energy worrying about her physical safety around male patrons who might want to "reform" her.

Discriminative perception is informed by examining the specific processes of oppression. For example, blacks or gays and lesbians may not be safe in the classroom because of the processes that systematically deny them voice, opportunity, and access. They are rendered invisible in urban classrooms where their life experiences are not discussed or are not even considered a possible topic for discussion. Even though black and gay and lesbian ghetto communities are visible in our urban centers, their place in urban higher education is still not secure. In addition, gay and lesbian people commonly lose their place in the class hierarchy if others learn of their sexual orientation (Johnson-Bailey and Cervero, 1998).

Power. Power and privilege are inextricably linked. Power forms the basis of privilege, and without power groups do not gain privilege. Force is an effective instrument for seizing and maintaining power and "remains the foundation of any system of inequality" (Lenski, 1986, p. 244), but it is less effective at retaining and exploiting a position of power. As Lenski (1986) writes, "*the ability to take life is the most effective form of power*" (p. 243, italics in original).

This coercive power is legitimatized through the law that "is identified with justice and the rule of right" (Lenski, 1986, p. 245). The general and impersonal terms used to write legislation seem to support abstract principles of justice, and laws can be written to "favor some particular segment of society" (p. 246). Coercive power is also legitimized through the manipulation of consensus by educational, religious, and other social institutions. By manipulating the law and consensus, the powerful shift the foundation of their power from force (or might) to justice (or right). Once power is established, it exists as the capacity to cause something to happen and as control over resources (Clegg, 1989).

The capacity to cause events and control resources becomes taken for granted by the dominant group, eventually evolving into a framework of social life that is "marked by stable, recurrent, patterned and cooperative interaction... within which orderly, explicable and facilitative uses of power might flourish" (Clegg, 1989, p. 131). These uses of power then contribute to "the general accomplishment of order and civility" (p. 131), which is necessary for the dominant group to enjoy unearned (and invisible to them/us) privilege.

Privilege. Discussions about privilege are predominately situated in the discourse of race (McIntosh, 1989; Scheurich, 1993). For instance, the realization that "white" is a culture, occurs "simultaneously with a negative connotation of privilege" (Frankenburg, 1993, p. 65) and a "location of structural advantage, of race privilege" (p. 1). Rocco and West (1998) have attempted to move the discussion on privilege beyond a single determinant of privilege—race—to a polyrhythmic view (Sheared, 1994) in which personal attributes function as determinants of privilege. These determinants are disability status, gender, religion, ethnicity, race, sexual orientation, age, and class.

If a person can "pass" for a member of the dominant culture on any one of these determinants, his or her experience of discriminatory situations is different than that of a person who cannot pass. Cultural imperialism creates the situation in which fear, guilt, or denial reflect the individual's perception of whether passing is right or wrong. Society's perception of the individual's privileged or marginalized status affects the power and privilege that might be enjoyed by or denied to the individual.

Our social system, then, is built on a foundation of coercive power that validates the legal system as based on what is in the best interest of the dominant group, which writes and enforces the law. This invisibility of privilege by those who are privileged leads to their belief that they are innocent and not complicit in the oppression of others. They view themselves and their actions as separate and independent, as not part of a group or social system, while simultaneously viewing members of oppressed groups as representatives of their group. This allows them to see affirmative action initiatives as disadvantaging the individual members of the dominant culture, who are worthy and capable and innocent of any overt racist acts.

An example is the Supreme Court case on the admissions policy of the University of Michigan in which the plaintiff sees the issue as a white woman being denied admission while less qualified black students were admitted. The plaintiff views "race" as the only category that honors race and considers the other items on the admissions list (which are highly correlated to the dominant white culture) to be race neutral categories, such as "legacy points" and "preparatory school points" (Smiley, 2003).

A Rudimentary Analysis of Antidiscrimination Law

In terms of discriminative justice, affirmative action, which is an example of positive discrimination, "assumes that the rights of the ethnic groups which the policy favors are of greater importance than the rights of either its individual members" or members of "groups not favored by the policy" (Bagnall, 1995, p. 85). Civil rights legislation is based on the premise that racism and discriminatory behavior are generally aberrations and that through measured steps we can create a fair and just society. Proponents of affirmative action view it as a proactive step that helps balance opportunities at work, in education, and in civil and social life. Those who are against affirmative action write that it "balkanizes the country, stigmatizes minorities, weakens the idea of merit, and constitutes reverse discrimination" (Delgado and Stefanic, 2001, p. 104). Examining affirmative action from the perspective of privilege, what is meritorious and worthy of reward is determined by those in the dominant group, who have regular and unfettered access to work, education, and civic and social opportunities. These same voices are not raised against white women, who as a group have received the most benefit from affirmative action policies (Guy-Sheftall, 1993, cited in Ladson-Billings, 2000). They see these women instead as meritorious, while ethnic and racial minorities or those whose sexual orientation is not heterosexual are viewed as beneficiaries of "special rights" (Anita Bryant, 1977, quoted in Bogert, 2002), which they neither deserve by virtue nor have earned through diligence.

Critical Race Theory. Critical race theory (CRT) is a movement that emerged from critical legal studies, an analysis of the law that questions "the very foundations of the liberal order, including equality theory, legal reasoning, Enlightenment rationalism, and neutral principles of constitutional law" (Delgado and Stefanic, 2001, p. 3). CRT begins with the notion of legal indeterminacy: the idea that legal cases can be decided in more than one way depending on which line of authority or interpretation of fact is emphasized. CRT has six themes:

1. Racism is endemic and ordinary.
2. Material determinism—our system of white over color—serves important material and psychic purposes.
3. Race is socially constructed.
4. Different minority groups are racialized at different times depending on economic need (a process known as differential racialization).
5. Individuals do not have unitary identities (a notion known as intersectionality and antiessentialism).
6. A unique voice of color that exists because of historical and current oppression can communicate to whites stories that whites are unlikely to know (Delgado and Stefanic, 2001).

These themes are not new to adult education or to those in urban communities whose experience exemplifies these themes.

According to CRT, the incremental change of affirmative action policies based on liberal ideals is achieving diminishing returns (Ladson-Billings, 2000), and whites are the principle beneficiaries of affirmative action. Affirmative action, the legal and social mandate to diversify the workforce so that instead of being predominately white men it resembles the community, benefits whites in two ways. First, affirmative action policies increase employment and advancement opportunities for white women; and second, these white women typically provide support for white families.

An example of these benefits can be seen in our medical and law schools. Of the 3,308 law-school graduates in the class of 1999 (comprising all degree-granting institutions), the largest minority group represented was white women, who composed 16 percent of the total. In this same graduating class, 3 percent were blacks and 2 percent were Hispanics (men and women) (National Center for Education Statistics, 2001). Another example can be seen in universities that reside in cities with a large population of blacks and classrooms dominated by white students.

CRT's Analysis of Discrimination. The concept of discrimination may be examined from the perspective of either the victim or the perpetrator (Freeman, 1995). From the victim perspective, discrimination will not be eliminated until the conditions associated with it are changed. The perpetrator perspective sees discrimination as a series of actions inflicted on the victim by the perpetrator. Perpetrators are "atomistic individuals whose actions are outside of and apart from the social fabric and without historical continuity" (Freeman, 1995, p. 30). In other words, current legal theory recognizes acts of discrimination as isolated events and as the misguided conduct of individuals. Antidiscrimination law is based on isolating the aberrant behaviors and outlawing them while doing nothing about the conditions that created discriminatory actions in the first place. If discriminatory action is treated as aberrant behavior (that is, if racism is seen as an isolated phenomenon), then the victim's condition cannot be changed, because society is denying the history, norms, and social policy that support discriminatory acts.

Two notions, fault and causation, are central to the perpetrator perspective. Under the notion of *fault*, the purpose of the law is to punish those individuals who are violating the shared societal norm of nondiscrimination. Discrimination is an intentional action accompanied by a desire to discriminate (Freeman, 1995). If someone can show that the discriminatory conduct was not intentional and was done for no good reason or for no reason at all, responsibility can be avoided. For instance, "[the fault concept] creates a class of 'innocents' who need not feel any personal responsibility for the conditions associated with discrimination" (Freeman, 1995, p. 30) and who are resentful of carrying any of the burdens associated with remedying discrimination.

The *causation* requirement separates the conditions that the law will address from the "totality of conditions that a victim perceives to be associated with discrimination" (Freeman, 1995, p. 30). Instances of discrimination can be seen as accidental if not linked to any apparent discriminatory effect. These two requirements—fault and causation—place the burden of proof on the victim, who must isolate the particular behavior and demonstrate intent.

This is evident in the current discussion about educational access and affirmative action policies: whites acknowledge that slavery occurred and was bad, yet do not accept any responsibility for something that occurred six generations ago. We conveniently forget that apartheid was the unwritten, and sometimes written, law of the land, creating separate educational systems, until the 1960s and 1970s. Forty years is not enough time to change the knowledge, meaning, and beliefs embedded in historical, social, and political systems.

Implications for Adult Education

If as adult educators we are hoping for a definitive guideline on when it is appropriate to discriminate against or discriminate in favor of certain categories of people, we must recognize the hidden and systemic nature of discrimination and realize how we participate in perpetuating discrimination. Discrimination based on race, sexual orientation, gender, and so on is ancient practice based on myths. As Montagu (1997, p. 41) writes, "A myth is a faulty explanation leading to social delusion and error, but we do not necessarily realize that we ourselves share in the mythmaking faculty with people of all times and places." These myths are an attempt to justify the inhumane and discriminatory treatment of one group by another group. Discrimination hides in myths, including the one that a discriminatory act is binary; it occurs or it does not.

The legal and political notions of discrimination do not account for its pervasive nature which cannot be condensed into a single isolated act or misguided conduct. As long as "discursive strategies… enable Whiteness to be positioned unquestioningly as the invisible norm, a norm that appears to have no tangible effects on pedagogy" (Shore, 2001, p. 43), discrimination is not and will not be a discrete act; instead it will be systemic. The assumptions and belief systems that allow us not to see or acknowledge that whiteness is the norm allow us to (mistakenly) think we can choose to discriminate or not to discriminate. The work of educators in urban universities is to examine our belief systems to see how we contribute to the oppression of others. We need to surface the actions and thoughts we have that support discrimination as a discrete act on an individual level and as part of institutional policy decisions. We further need to explore how our thoughts and actions support discriminatory systems that privilege straight, white, Christian people over all others and thereby suppress the inherent complexity of urban life. The geographic location of urban institutions does not guarantee a welcoming and nurturing environment for all adult learners. Urban higher education institutions are created in the image of higher education to serve and support the privileged white, middle-class male. We need to ask, Do we welcome the children of our students in our classrooms? Probing further, does the institute maintain affordable, available child care for caregiver parents (Bailey-Iddrisu, 2002)?

Even if we work hard to eradicate discrimination, we will continue to commit acts of discrimination daily because as whites we assume no individual or collective responsibility for the discrimination that occurs today or for past racist acts. After all, many of us are descendants of immigrants and therefore not responsible, we believe. As long as we see discrimination as isolated, regrettable, individual acts, urban centers will not change. For example, many faculty search committees lament the lack of qualified minority candidates. The committee members view this lack as the result of negligence and lack of support on the part of faculty at other institutions for minority students, or the fault of a public educational system that has failed to educate potential scholars. We do not recognize the systems we have in place, which operate to deter bright potential scholars of color and racialized others from applying or pursuing doctorates. For instance, an urban university designated a historical minority university recently raised the GRE score for admission consideration to 1120, recognizing in its policy document that GRE scores are not good indicators of academic success for minority and nontraditional students. This university's student body consists of more than 50 percent minority students, yet the administration has failed to see this policy as discriminatory, instead choosing to believe that it is a neutral act designed simply to improve the university's standing in the *Princeton Review.*

So, the question for adult educators might be, When is discrimination good? Discrimination is good when it builds people's capacity to choose freely where to live, where to work, and with whom to associate (Sen, 1999). Discriminative action is good when it reveals processes of oppression and privilege in classrooms, funding, and policies. Adult educators must struggle to recognize the small things we do that honor this system that privileges some and marginalizes others. We should attempt to deconstruct the dynamics in the classroom and in the boardroom that replicate oppression.

Adult educators must work to surface the complexities of the diverse experiences represented by multiple groups and not just focus on the historical division between black and white (Moses, 2002) that can affect the learning environment. A characteristic of urban living is diversity and the complexity that results from it (Daley, Fisher, and Martin, 2000). Knowledge construction in urban adult education must affirm complex new relations and dynamics and discriminate against the simplistic, binary construction of knowledge. For example, not all blacks associate with the history of discrimination in this country. For example, people of color who recently came to this country from the Caribbean Islands see the opportunity and advantages in an urban setting. Knowledge-construction processes in urban adult education need to allow this complexity to shape educational discourse.

References

Bagnall, R. "Discriminative Justice and Responsibility in Postmodern Adult Education." *Adult Education Quarterly,* 1995, 45(2), 79–94.

Bailey-Iddrisu, V. "University Policies Which Serve to Increase/Decrease Access for African-American Women." In N. Ray, J. Johnson-Bailey, and M. C. Burke (eds.), *Proceedings of the Tenth Annual African American Adult Education Research Pre-Conference.* Athens: University of Georgia, May 2002.

Bauman, Z. *Postmodernity: Chance or Menace?* Lancaster, U.K.: Centre for the Study of Cultural Values, 1991.

Bell, D. *Faces at the Bottom of the Well.* New York: Basic Books, 1992.

Bogert, N. *The Gay Rights Fight: Then and Now—Then: Anita Bryant Brought Celebrity to Fight; Now: Most Oppose Appeal.* Internet Broadcasting Systems, Inc. [http://www.nbc6.net/News/1651594/detail.html], Sept. 5, 2002.

Cervero, R. M., and Wilson, A. L. (eds.). *Power in Practice: Adult Education and the Struggle for Knowledge and Power in Society.* San Francisco: Jossey-Bass, 2001.

Clegg, S. R. *Frameworks of Power.* London: Sage, 1989.

Cornell, S., and Hartmann, D. *Ethnicity and Race: Making Identities in a Changing World.* Thousand Oaks, Calif.: Pine Forge Press, 1998.

Daley, B. J., Fisher, J. C., and Martin, L. G. "Urban Contexts for Adult Education Practice." In A. Wilson and E. Hayes (eds.), *Handbook of Adult and Continuing Education.* San Francisco: Jossey-Bass, 2000.

Delgado, R., and Stefanic, J. *Critical Race Theory: An Introduction.* New York: New York University Press, 2001.

Eckert, P. C. *Jocks and Burnouts: Social Categories and Identity in the High School.* New York: Teachers College, Columbia University, 1989.

Frankenburg, R. *The Social Construction of Whiteness: White Women, Race Matters.* Minneapolis: University of Minnesota Press, 1993.

Freeman, A. D. "Legitimizing Racial Discrimination Through Antidiscrimination Law: A Critical Review of Supreme Court Doctrine." In K. Crenshaw, N. Gotanda, G. Peller, and K. Thomas (eds.), *Critical Race Theory: The Key Writings That Formed the Movement.* New York: New Press, 1995.

Goffman, E. *Stigma: Notes on the Management of Spoiled Identity.* New York: Simon & Schuster, 1963.

Guy-Sheftall, B. "Black Feminist Perspectives on the Academy." Paper presented at the annual meeting of the American Educational Research Association, Atlanta, Apr. 1993.

Johnson-Bailey, J., and Cervero, R. M. "Power Dynamics in Teaching and Learning Practices: An Examination of Two Adult Education Classrooms." *International Journal of Lifelong Education,* 1998, *17*(6), 389–399.

Ladson-Billings, G. "Racialized Discourses and Ethnic Epistemologies." In N. K. Denzin and Y. S. Lincoln (eds.), *The Handbook of Qualitative Research* (2nd ed.) Thousand Oaks, Calif.: Sage, 2000.

Lenski, G. "Power and Privilege." In S. Lukes (ed.), *Power.* New York: New York University Press, 1986. (Originally published 1966.)

McIntosh, P. "White Privilege: Unpacking the Invisible Knapsack." *Peace and Freedom,* 1989, *49*(4), 10–12.

Montagu, A. *Man's Most Dangerous Myth: The Fallacy of Race* (6th ed.). Walnut Creek, Calif.: AltaMira Press, 1997. (Originally published 1942.)

Moses, M. S. *Embracing Race: Why We Need Race-Education Policy.* New York: Teachers College Press, 2002.

National Center for Education Statistics. "Chapter 3: Postsecondary Education." *Digest of Education Statistics, 2001.* Washington, D.C.: National Center for Education Statistics, 2001.

Peterson, E. "Creating a Culturally Relevant Dialogue for African American Adult Educators." In T. C. Guy (ed.), *Providing Culturally Relevant Adult Education: A Challenge for the Twenty-First Century.* New Directions for Adult and Continuing Education, no. 82. San Francisco: Jossey-Bass, 1999.

Pharr, S. *Homophobia: A Weapon of Sexism.* San Francisco: Chardon Press, 1988.

Rocco, T. S., and West, G. W. "Deconstructing Privilege: An Examination of Privilege in Adult Education." *Adult Education Quarterly,* 1998, *48*(3), 171–184.

Scheurich, J. J. "Toward a Discourse on White Racism." *Educational Researcher,* 1993, *22*(8), 5–10.

Sen, A. *Development as Freedom.* New York: Anchor Books, 1999.

Sheared, V. "Giving Voice: An Inclusive Model of Instruction—A Womanist Perspective." In E. Hayes and S.A.J. Colin III (eds.), *Confronting Racism and Sexism.* New Directions for Adult and Continuing Education, no. 61. San Francisco: Jossey-Bass, 1994.

Sheared, V. "Giving Voice: Inclusion of African American Students' Polyrhythmic Realities in Adult Basic Education." In T. C. Guy (ed.), *Providing Culturally Relevant Adult Education: A Challenge for the Twenty-First Century.* New Directions for Adult and Continuing Education, no. 82. San Francisco: Jossey-Bass, 1999.

Shore, S. "Talking about Whiteness: 'Adult Learning Principles' and the Invisible Norm." In V. Sheared and P. A. Sissel (eds.), *Making Space: Merging Theory and Practice in Adult Education.* Westport, Conn.: Bergin & Garvey, 2001.

Smiley, T. *The Tavis Smiley Show*. Washington, D.C.: National Public Radio and the African American Consortium, Feb. 7, 2003. Radio broadcast.

Swigonski, M. E., Mama, R. S., and Ward, K. (eds.). *From Hate Crimes to Human Rights: A Tribute to Matthew Shepard*. Binghamton, N.Y.: Haworth Press, 2001.

Webster's New Explorer Dictionary and Thesaurus. Springfield, Mass.: Federal Street Press, 1999.

Young, I. M. *Justice and the Politics of Difference*. Princeton, N.J.: Princeton University Press, 1990.

TONETTE S. ROCCO is assistant professor of adult education and human resource development at Florida International University.

SUZANNE J. GALLAGHER is a doctoral candidate in adult education and human resource development at Florida International University.

4

Adult education instructors and administrators, who typically are not members of the hip-hop generation, have little or no background, sensitivity, or understanding of the influence and significance of black popular culture and music for young African American and white adult learners.

Gangsta Rap and Adult Education

Talmadge C. Guy

They call it the Rhythm Nation, the hip-hop generation, and bling-bling culture. They celebrate thuggin' and pimpin'. Their mottos are "keep it real" and "getting paid." For many adult educators, these terms are shocking and removed from their personal experiences and cultural backgrounds. Hip-hop culture pervades almost every aspect of modern urban adolescent and young adult life in America. But hip-hop music and culture and their more explicit and shocking expression, gangsta rap, are more than a passing adolescent excursion into self-discovery and a rebellion against an older generation. I argue that the impact of hip-hop culture and gangsta rap music on adult education is becoming more evident in urban environments as more and more young adults enter adult education programs and bring hip-hop and gangsta rap influences into the classroom.

Yet the rise of hip-hop and gangsta rap is significantly the result of the sponsorship and control of black artists by the major music media corporations who promote and distribute the music. This relationship between rap and hip-hop artists and the major media is fundamentally an exploitive one in which white corporations profit from promoting selected black artists and themes: "The six major record firms have a quasi-colonial relationship with the black Rhythm Nation of America that produces hip-hop and other forms of black music. Despite the names of a few big money-makers—Suge Knight, Sean Combs, and Russell Simmons… rap, like most black music, is under the corporate control of whites and purchased mostly by whites" (Kelly, 1999). This relationship produces a vibrant, seductive art form, but also promotes sexism, violence, materialism, and instant gratification at the expense of the educational impulse in African American urban communities. This is apparent in the Wu-Tang Clan's mega hit "C.R.E.A.M.," an acronym that stands for "Cash Rules Everything Around Me," and in

N.W.A.'s (Niggaz With Attitude) "Gangsta Gangsta" and "Fuck the Police" (Werner, 1998). Because the media serve as powerful agents for the dissemination of messages about identity, place, and society (Kellner, 1995), it is imperative that adult educators understand the influence of hip-hop and gangsta rap on adults in urban adult education programs. Adult education practitioners working in an urban context increasingly encounter learners who are influenced by this black urban culture, and they unwittingly serve the interests of the white capitalist culture industry by reinforcing stereotypes of black adults as dysfunctional, antisocial, irrational, and self-consumed when they ignore the effect of "gangsta rap" and culture on the experiences of African American learners.

In this chapter I explore this effect using the concept of the city as educational agent (Negre and Bernet, 1993). From a sociocultural perspective, I outline the ways in which the city's racialized structure influences the cultural production, commodification, and consumption of African American popular culture, especially as exemplified through hip-hop and gangsta rap music as the dominant form of black urban cultural expression. I conclude with a presentation of some implications of African American culture as influenced by the culture industry for adult education and learning within the African American urban community.

African Americans: The Urban Experience

African American urban experience can be understood as a complex mixture of opportunity and advancement situated in the experience of oppression and marginalization. It is impossible to understand the cultural experience of African Americans in the modern American city without also understanding how racism functions to segregate, isolate, and denigrate black identity and culture. In asserting this latter point, it is important to specify that urban African American spaces not only represent physical locations but also are conceptualized as existing in relation to white spaces in ways that privilege whites (Haymes, 1995).

This conception of African American urban space invokes two related meanings. In the first sense, *urban space* refers to the ways that African Americans are segregated into particular communities and prevented from moving beyond them as a result of institutionalized policies and practices that seek to separate and preserve preferred areas for whites (Massey and Denton, 1993). In the second sense, the ability to define and enforce designated black spaces is linked to the exercise of economic, political, and social power. Thus, the power to differentiate black spaces from white spaces through legal, economic, and political means constitutes a real and fundamental goal of racist ideology.

Within this context of clearly defined African American urban space, African American music has reflected the complex and multidimensional nature of urban life. Sheared (1994, p. 28) has presented the idea that African American cultural reality is best understood through the concept of "polyrhythm." This idea emphasizes the intersection of multiple rhythms—spiritual, economic, communal, and sensual—that permeate the African American experience. Thus, spirituals, gospel, the blues, jazz, rhythm and blues, and now hip-hop and gangsta rap are musical idioms that reflect the multiplicity and complexity of African American culture and life. The emergence and development of African American urban culture and identity are closely linked to the establishment of African American urban spaces and reflect the themes of African American experience in hypersegregated and racialized urban settings.

The Emergence of the Black Ghetto

The years 1900, 1950, and 2000 represent distinct and significant points in time that frame a discussion about the nature and quality of life of blacks in America. According to the *Statistical Atlas of the United States Based on the Eleventh Census* of 1890 (Gannett, 1898), fewer than 10 percent of blacks[1] lived outside the South. Between 1900 and 1910, approximately 197,000 blacks moved out of the South to northern cities (Massey and Denton, 1993). Between 1910 and 1920 the number rose to 525,000, and by 1930 it reached 825,000 (Massey and Denton, 1993). The primary impetus for the increase was the lure of work.

During the 1940s and 1950s, African Americans continued to move out of the South to the North, Midwest, and West in large numbers as the invention and use of the mechanical cotton picker and the South's full economic recovery from the Civil War eliminated the need for widespread use of share-cropping, which had been the primary source of employment for African Americans since the days of reconstruction (Franklin, 1969). By 1950, the proportion of blacks living in the North had risen to 40 percent (Fitzsimmons, 1950; Hounsel, 2003). The number of blacks moving out of the South increased to 1.5 million persons in the 1950s and 1.4 million during the 1960s (Massey and Denton, 1993).

Between 1950 and 2000, significant social changes associated with the civil rights movement and the outlawing of de jure segregation affected the lives of African Americans. Significant shifts in population centers were realized during these years as African Americans completed the migration to the northern cities from the southern rural and agricultural areas. The messianic vision of the free North and the hopefulness of the civil rights movement, however, have since been overshadowed by the poverty, despair, isolation, and crime of black urban centers. As a group, African Americans have realized few of the progressive ideals associated with life in the modern American city (Jeffries, 1998).

The Black Metropolis

The promise of opportunity and advancement lured many southern blacks to northern cities, yet the story of black Americans and the city is actually a complex interweaving of themes of hope and tragedy, prosperity and poverty, survival and death, community and crass individualism. On the one hand, large black communities became home to an intellectual and cultural outpouring and expressiveness. In the 1920s in Harlem, New York, for example, the New Negro Movement and the poets, writers, and artists of the Harlem Renaissance redefined the meaning of *Negro* through the cultural expressions of art, drama, poetry, and music (Locke, 1925). Northern urban communities spawned intellectual and social protest movements and became home to a growing number of African American intellectuals and scholars, such as W.E.B. Du Bois, Alain Locke, Ralph Bunche, Zora Neale Hurston, Carter G. Woodson, Marcus Garvey, Richard Wright, Jessie Fauset, Nella Larsen, and Walter White, to name just a few. In referring to the center of the black urban experience, Langston Hughes's (1965) famous character Jesse B. Semple captured the spirit of the new black metropolis:

Here's to Harlem!
They say Heaven is Paradise
If Harlem ain't Heaven
Then a mouse ain't mice!

While many African Americans prospered, the mushrooming of the black population in cities led to reactionary strategies by whites to disenfranchise and isolate blacks within racially segregated communities. As the number of blacks in northern cities grew, the development of ghetto inner cities transformed the urban landscape (Bennett, 1974; Franklin, 1969). In their classic study of black Chicago, St. Clair Drake and Horace Cayton (1962, p. 79) describe how white Chicagoans used violence as well as legal means to restrict the location and movement of African Americans:

> In one block on Michigan Avenue, a synagogue bought by a Negro Baptist congregation was repeatedly bombed in 1925. (The colored congregation ultimately took out an insurance policy against bombing.)... To deny living space to Negroes, law-abiding white Chicagoans developed something more subtle than a "pineapple" tossed by a "gorilla" hired by a respectable "neighborhood improvement association". In the spring of 1928, the Hyde Park Herald, a neighborhood newspaper, reported a speech proclaiming the efficacy of a new device for locking Negroes within the Black Belt.

Known as the *restricted covenant,* this legal device was used to ensure that a property owner would agree "not to exchange with, sell to, or lease to any member of a race not Caucasian" (Drake and Cayton, 1962). In fact, the National Association of Real Estate Brokers adopted as part of its code of ethics a statement prohibiting realtors from integrating neighborhoods, which might lower property values (Massey and Denton, 1993).

Discrimination in housing was accompanied by denial of service at restaurants and other public establishments (Franklin, 1969; Massey and Denton, 1993). Employment discrimination was widespread and blacks often found it difficult to obtain bank loans. African American males were frequently harassed by the police and subject to arrest if caught in a white neighborhood. Thus, the emergence of the black metropolis was accompanied by a growing white backlash aimed at limiting and segregating blacks.

Black Strivings and Faltering Expectations

Historian Lerone Bennett (1968) has argued that the emergence and growth of the black metropolis rested largely on the maintenance of a stable economic base. For African Americans arriving in northern and Midwestern cities in the 1920s, 1930s, and 1940s, jobs were plentiful, albeit low paying and involving menial labor. This meant that African American workers and families in the North and Midwest could at least have an economic situation that compared favorably with that of the agricultural South. Beginning in the 1960s, this economic base began to collapse with the accelerating departure of industrial firms in the aftermath of urban unrest, urban renewal, and increasing pressure from competitive international companies (Bennett, 1974). As a consequence, African American workers found it increasingly difficult to find and keep stable and relatively well-paying jobs.

With the decline of the economic base of the black inner city, middle-class African Americans who had the money to afford housing in suburban areas found new opportunities for employment and residence and increasingly chose to live in suburbs that previously had been limited to whites. The flight of the African American middle class to the suburbs constituted in a real sense an abandonment of the black metropolis, which left the black inner city poor, destitute, and susceptible to murder, drugs, and prostitution (Wilson, 1987). Thus, urban African American communities became increasingly isolated, detached, poor, welfare-dependent, and infested with gang warfare, drugs, unemployment, and single-family households.

The frustrations of large numbers of African Americans trapped in urban ghettos produced the environment in which the urban uprisings of the 1960s occurred. The Kerner Commission on Civil Disorders (1968), impaneled by President Johnson to investigate widespread urban unrest, asserted that there were two Americas—black and white—and they were unequal. Despite legal and policy initiatives such as affirmative action, urban redevelopment, model cities programs, economic empowerment zones, and compensatory social and educational programs such as Adult Basic Education and Head Start, by the 1990s American cities were highly stratified in terms of income levels, employment, and educational attainment and remained divided and unequal. By 1990, income for black households was 58 percent of income for white households, blacks were twice as likely as whites to drop out of high school, and black households were three times more likely than white households to have one wage earner (Hacker, 1992).

Orlando Patterson's assessment of the effects of the civil rights movement on black life argues that while African Americans have made tremendous progress in education, employment, and income since 1970, African Americans are still three times as likely to be poor and twice as likely to be unemployed (Patterson, 1997). Bennett (1968) poignantly characterizes this situation in noting that "freedom divorced from an economic foundation, freedom divorced from the wherewithal, cannot guarantee anything except the freedom to talk or the freedom to starve" (p. 286)—and a highly stylized, often confrontational, always-hip black talk developed in the culture of the urban black ghetto.

It is not difficult, then, to understand the development of the rebellious, oppositional, discourse-based musical genre reflected in the lyricism of the blues, R&B, and rap. In the midst of this social, cultural, political, and economic segregation, black urban culture emerged—initially as a vibrant expression of black political and cultural strivings. The following section describes the development of what is now recognized as the genesis of African American culture in the twentieth century.

Black Urban Popular Culture and Cultural Production

Music, the lifeblood of black expressive culture has been transfigured by the rap revolution. From its beginnings in the black urban realities of New York in the 1970s, rap has transcended the boundaries of the 'hood to become an international force in popular and capitalist culture (Gilroy, 1998). Rap music has become a multimillion-dollar industry generating billions of dollars in sales and with a global marketing reach (Cashmore, 1997; Kelly, 1999). It appeals to a broad, multiracial, multiethnic, multinational market, two-thirds of whom are white and spend nearly two billion dollars a year (Kelly, 1999).

Rap music's appeal stems from the lines and cadences uttered by quintessential black urban young adults whose distinctive and patterned ways of "behaving, interacting, valuing, thinking, believing, and speaking"(Gee, 1996) reflect a place that stands in opposition to and in defiance of mainstream, middle-class, white standards, values, and norms (Fordham, 1999). While it is an outgrowth of black cultural traditions, its particular force is rooted in the "postindustrial transformation of urban life, and the contemporary technological terrain" (Rose, 1994) that foregrounds materialism, consumerism, and the high-tech graphic images seen in music videos on cable stations such as MTV and VH1. The ear-shattering, bone-rattling bass lines of rap music can be heard emanating from electronic music systems through loudspeakers located in the trunks of cars driven through the streets of almost any major American city.

Emphasizing themes of sadness, anger, despair, sexuality, and survival, rap's cultural roots in blues, jazz, and R&B are evident (Werner, 1998). As Chuck D, former leader of rap group N.W.A., said in a recent interview, hip-hop began with an emphasis on "knowledge of self" and connection to "community, family, and love" (Hounsel, 2003). Yet young adolescent males whose cultural memory is as long as their middle fingers do not make the connection between self and race, individual and community, improvisation and cultural connectedness that earlier cultural representatives—Bessie Smith, Louis Armstrong and Ella Fitzgerald; Billie Holliday and Dizzy Gille-spie; Miles Davis and Sarah Vaughn; the Supremes and the Temptations; James Brown and Aretha Franklin—did. When Billie Holliday sang "God Bless the Child That's Got Its Own," all black people could relate—rich and poor, city and country, working and unemployed (Floyd, 1995). When James Brown sang "Say It Loud, I'm Black and I'm Proud!" he energized a collective consciousness for social protest and race advancement (Cash-more, 1997). African American music—touching the depths of the soul—simultaneously translated and transmitted a messianic and transcendent message of hope while maintaining a centeredness in urban black realities.

The political and economic reality is that access to the mainstream brings wealth and fame but requires that black artists yield control of their music to the hegemony of a white-owned, white-run black culture indus-try. This system operates in a subtle and insidious way. Mass consumer needs are produced through the manipulation of powerful cultural symbols that are cleverly manipulated and manufactured (Adorno and Horkheimer, 1991). In culture industries it is argued that consumers' needs are satisfied through the intelligent operation of market forces. The satisfaction of con-sumers' needs leads to the growth of profit by capitalist organizations. The consequence is that a cycle of need satisfaction and need manipulation strengthens the culture industry that seeks further to manipulate and con-trol in search of profit.

A central aspect of this system is that only those people with sufficient economic power have the ability to manipulate consumer needs and create and expand markets in the first place. These white-owned and -run com-panies do not operate in the interests of black urban communities seeking to reverse decades of racist segregation and disenfranchisement. Instead, these culture industries operate in the interests of their owners and the white community of which they are a part. The African American commu-nity becomes the market that produces profit. Even black owned and oper-ated labels such as Death Row, Bad Boy Entertainment, and Def Jam Records have been financed and controlled by white media megacorporations such as Polygram, CBS's Epic Records, MCA Music, and Warner (Kelly, 1999).

In its early stages, rap music constituted a strong countercritique of white racism. This critical dimension has been eclipsed, however, as rap and rappers have become engulfed by the lure of money fed through the pipeline of the major media corporations. Resistant to protest against rap's violence and misogyny from within the African American community as well as from the government, black popular cultural icons have gained popularity as they have increasingly been identified as antisocial. It is important to understand that support for black gangsta rap came through major media labels who were interested in marketing entertainment and selling records to a growing audience of both black and white listeners. Cultural critic Michael Eric Dyson has noted that young African American males can easily get an album made if they are telling a story about how hard the ghetto is rather than fighting white racism (Dyson, 1996).

Boyd (1997) refers to two generations of black rappers. The first generation he calls "affirmative action" rappers. Affirmative action rappers were influenced by a social context framed by the civil rights and Black Power movements of the 1960s and 1970s. The later (and current) generation of rappers he calls "Reagonomic" rappers. These rappers were influenced by the harsh social and economic consequences of the conservative Reagan presidency. Reagonomic rappers saw and responded to a context of increasing victimization and marginalization of African Americans, for whom the realization of the American dream seemed increasingly remote. As a consequence, Reagonomic rappers strive for self-aggrandizement for the sake of community advancement. Nihilism and self-hatred have become endemic in black popular music in particular and black urban culture in general.

Writer and cultural critic Sherley Ann Williams (1998, p. 167) comments about rap, "Black people have to ask ourselves why so much of it has become so vehemently misogynistic, violent, and sexually explicit, so soaked in black self hatred?" She asks for a critical examination of popular black culture, especially as expressed through music, so that we "understand the distinction between the rock and what lives under it—and what ought to die when it's exposed to the light of day" (p. 168). Rap has lost its political and cultural edge and is now largely conformist within American culture. In practical terms, this suggests that black popular culture no longer serves as a means for cultural or political critique and transformation. Instead, rap music serves to reinforce white racist attitudes and to domesticate black creative tension. Ellis Cashmore (1997, p. 171) says it plainly: "Rap transformed racism into fashion: something that blacks wore to impress and whites liked to glare at without actually doing anything; both virtually countenanced it, at the same time keeping their distance from one another. What started as a radically different and, in many ways, dangerous music was appropriated, domesticated and ultimately rendered harmless."

Urban Cultures at the Crossroads:
Race and Urban Space

In the pursuit of a vibrant urban cultural life, African Americans have pursued many avenues to ease the problems associated with urban life. At times this pursuit has led to seeking the good life at the expense of other black people (Jeffries, 1998). An important vehicle in the pursuit of material comfort has been the anonymity afforded urban residents. It is easy to shelter one's identity in a densely crowded and impersonal urban setting. This has been especially true for those in search of a "hip, cool, got it going on" lifestyle—the essence of which is the economic independence to be as expressively free and unconstrained as possible, especially in light of the larger, hostile white community.

The reality of black urban life, however, has been that all aspects of black life have been circumscribed by the larger community. Richard Wright (2001, p. 23) captured this sentiment in his classic, *Native Son:* "Look! We live here and they live there. We black and they white. They got things and we ain't. They do things and we can't." The inescapable reality of racist policies and practices have been as prevalent in the city as they were in the Jim Crow South.

The clearly carved spatial separation of black and white communities have been made real by the economic policies and practices of the insurance and banking industry, which has practiced "redlining." Segregated communities have provided security and a sense of normalcy for whites. Clearly defined African American neighborhoods have provided a means for surveillance and control by the police and city officials. Clearly defined African American neighborhoods provide a map for the distribution of social and economic goods throughout the city (Massey and Denton, 1993).

Despite the disparities between the black and white communities, pathways through the city converge and provide places for people to interact. Thus, while urban black cultural expressions such as rap and hip-hop are rooted in black urban reality, whites share in this cultural expression by patronizing establishments that sponsor black musicians (Jeffries, 1998). White youth "cross over" to black music by buying the music of black artists (Cashmore, 1997) and thus are entertained and titillated by rap and hip-hop. As the groundswell of white demand for black culture increases, the contact between street elements of African American communities and white youth also increases. Terms such as *wigger* are amicably used to designate white lovers of black culture and music. This contact, however, is carefully choreographed because the rules of racial engagement make it impossible for whites and blacks to establish genuine long-lasting relationships that extend beyond the bounds of entertainment and play.

Thus, questions arise: What is black urban culture? Who owns it? Who creates and who produces it? Answers to these questions become central to understanding the experiences of young adults in urban America, who come from a range of urban community contexts but share a common pain and angst over their diminished life chances. As Fine and Weis (1998, p. 11) have conveyed in their study of urban, poor, working-class young adults, "The language of pain and possibility circulates up and down the northeast corridor, in code switching from Latino dialects to black vernacular to white slang."

Despite the context that shapes the perspective of urban black youth, a fundamental issue is the way in which gangsta rap and hip-hop culture—at least the more virulent strains of them—celebrate black-on-black violence. As Williams (1998, p. 171) makes clear:

> Rappers' fantasies about killing white people, in general, or policemen in particular, are no more than the letting off of steam about the almost unbearable racist pressure under which most of us live: these fantasies are not the ones that are acted upon. Black male homicide rates are not the highest in the country because these young men decided to take out a cop or some white person. Those rates are created by black men offing each other. No, it's the so-called fantasies about pulling "a trigger on some nigger" that concern me, the ones about the "gang-banging 'ho" and the "ghetto bitch" the rapper feels perfectly justified in "stickin dick" to that frighten me. These are the realities I see enacted in the streets in my part of the city [emphasis in original].

It is this brutal reality that educators of urban adults confront as they go to work in black urban communities. As a number of scholars have observed, urban black youth increasingly reject formal education as "acting white" (Bergin and Cooks, 2002; Fordham and Ogbu, 1986). In a study of predominately African American adult basic education (ABE) classrooms I learned that there is a serious and growing gap between older African American adults who take seriously the learning opportunities available to them in adult education programs and young adult learners who reject formal adult education programs. This gap is so large that it actually leads to conflict between students who see themselves as members of the hip-hop culture and students who do not (Guy, 2003).

Finally, adult education instructors are confounded by the perceived callous and relaxed attitude of hip-hop adults toward adult education. Instructors are typically unprepared to interact with these learners who speak and act toward them in ways that can best be characterized as denigrating and demeaning.

Representing Blackness: The City as Educational Agent

Negre and Bernet (1993, p. 17) offer the concept of the city as an agent of education, as an "educative context." In their view, the city is a source of learning and socialization for its residents. In particular, the organization and allocation of social spaces conveys knowledge and information about the city, the people who live there, and the larger society in which it is located. Given their racial and ethnic mixture of peoples, urban spaces provide for the possibility of a multicultural interweaving of peoples and histories. A dense urban population fosters communicative opportunities and the possibility for the combination of some cultural elements in new and unforeseen ways. Stadiums, cinemas, malls, parks, and music auditoriums create crossroads where city dwellers occupying different spaces can interact and "cross borders" (Giroux and McLaren, 1994, p. 2). As a complex network of human relations, the city also has an educative and socializing effect on its residents.

But cities are also ambivalent in regard to this educative function. It may be desirable to see the city as the place to learn civility and good taste; it is also idealistic. Negre and Bernet (1993) argue that the city in fact fosters "aggressiveness, marginalization, insensitivity, over consumption, and indifference" and therefore diminishes, trivializes, commodifies, and demonizes minority cultures along with the people who consume, generate, and identify with that culture. So, while the city provides the opportunity for persons of racially and culturally diverse backgrounds to intermingle and communicate, the pattern for most inner-city African Americans is that this opportunity is seldom realized.

In a general sense, then, white knowledge about black culture and identity is not the result of direct personal interaction or even of indirect contact through vicariously lived experiences with African Americans. As Lukes (1973) points out, knowledge draws on concepts and categories that are collective representations of symbolic forms that members of a social group both cognize and communicate. White conceptions of blackness result from internalizing the cultural representations of black bodies and spaces, and white corporate media are the major source of conceptual representations of blackness.

The conceptual and ideological dimensions of this process are important to understand. Whiteness becomes a synonym for order, reason, and boundedness (Rodriguez, 1998). Black culture becomes synonymous with disorderliness, irrationality, and danger. Black culture is to be controlled, and if this cannot be completely achieved, it is to be isolated, segregated, and confined. Media representations of blackness portray black identity and black culture as out of control and needing to be eradicated from the cosmopolitan urban environment. The images of thug "gangstas" on many rap compact disk covers suggest not only the rebellious black male but also the out-of-control and dangerous black male. Such images become models for African American youth to emulate and for white youth to impersonate.

Thus, urban adult education is imprinted with and shaped by the cultural and ideological representations of blackness in the development and delivery of programs and services. We see this in every attempt to broaden the scope of educational activity to become more culturally relevant to the needs and aspirations of the different communities in the city. The conceptualization of blackness as degenerate, maladaptive, and dysfunctional gives support to educational initiatives that valorize Eurocentrism and whiteness. Urban adult education programs, especially those with government or corporate support, do not address the complex reality of the black urban experience. The rancorous debate over the Oakland school board's adoption of an Ebonics policy, triggered by the widely held but incorrect view that black English is not a legitimate dialect but an aberrant form of English (Guy, 1999), or the adoption of welfare reform in the mid-1990s based on media-driven assessments that welfare recipients are black, lazy, and immoral (Sheared, 2001) are but two examples of the way media-driven conceptualizations of blackness have influenced public policy and adult education.

Critical Media Literacy and Agency in Adult Education

In connecting black popular music to the work of adult educators, the central problem is to create a sense of agency and efficacy to combat the racist effects of the media on urban education. Confronted with assimilationist and color-blind approaches to adult education, urban learners in adult education fail to be challenged through critical consideration of the way their lives are constructed through the process of allocating urban spaces.

Several scholars have developed analyses that assert the critical and radically transformative potential of hip-hop and rap music. From their perspective, rap music is grounded in resistance and oppositional identity politics (McCarthy, 1999; Rose, 1994; McLaren, 1999), critical and antiracist analysis (Haymes, 1995; Paul, 2000), and social movement politics (Haymes, 1995; Rose, 1994). These arguments have some merit, with the emphasis on *potential*. But a distinction must be made between popular culture that possesses a political message rooted in African American sociocultural reality and rap that enacts a consumerist, materialist, sexist, violent, and pornographic worldview. The potential for fostering learner agency lies in the former, not the latter. As a matter of fact, the conversion of black cultural critique into mass-produced commodities for mass consumption undermines any potential for radical critique. Therefore, a culturally relevant black pedagogy must confront the context in which black popular culture is produced as well as its product—namely, the negative messages in its content. Such a strategy forms the basis for a critical and effective urban pedagogy. Haymes (1995, p. 145) says, "A pedagogy of black urban struggle linked to a representational pedagogy would recognize that black self-contempt is the result of blacks essentializing or biologizing their bodies, using white supremacist definitions of race and blackness."

Adult education instructors and administrators, who typically are not members of the hip-hop generation, have little or no background in, sensitivity to, or understanding of the influence and significance of black popular culture and music for young African American and white adult learners. In the context of ABE, Amstutz (2001) argues that this situation is characteristic of a broader "cultural gap" that exists between adult education staff and adult learners in ABE. It is my view that as long as a cultural gap exists between professional, paid, and volunteer providers of adult education working in urban contexts and their students, the needs of adult learners will not be met.

I therefore believe that it is essential to promote critical media literacy among adult educators as an important first step in addressing the complex and adverse influences of gangsta rap and hip-hop on adult learners in adult education classrooms. Black learners who have internalized the negative messages often lack interest in pursuing education at all, and white and black adult educators often hold negative and stereotypical views of black learners that interfere with their ability to meet learners' needs.

Creating cultural crossroads within adult classrooms makes it possible to critically challenge the assumptions that underlie the co-optation and production of black popular cultural expressions. But the decision to engage cross-cultural spaces in an urban context must be made with a clear political goal of combating the effects of racism that ultimately adversely affect all segments of the city.

Notes

1. The term *colored* was in use at the time of the 1890 census and included blacks, Chinese, Japanese, and Indians. Thus, comparisons across decades must be understood in the context of the changing definitions of demographic designations.

References

Adorno, T. W., and Horkheimer, M. "The Culture Industry: Enlightenment and Mass Deception." In T. W. Adorno and J. M. Bernstein (eds.), *The Culture Industry: Selected Essays on Mass Culture.* London: Routledge, 1991.

Amstutz, D. "Adult Basic Education: Equipped for the Future or for Failure?" In V. Sheared and P. A. Sissel (eds.), *Making Space: Merging Theory and Practice in Adult Education.* Westport, Conn.: Bergin and Garvey, 2001.

Bennett, L. *Confrontation: Black and White.* (2nd ed.) Baltimore: Penguin, 1968.

Bennett, L. *The Shaping of Black America.* Chicago: Johnson, 1974.

Bergin, D. A., and Cooks, H. C. "High School Students of Color Talk About Accusations of 'Acting White.'" *Urban Review,* 2002, 34(2), 13-34.

Boyd, T. *Am I Black Enough for You? Popular Culture from the 'Hood and Beyond.* Bloomington: Indiana University Press, 1997.

Cashmore, E. *The Black Culture Industry.* London: Routledge, 1997.

Drake, S. C., and Cayton, H. R. *Black Metropolis: A Study of Negro Life in a Northern City* (rev. ed.) New York: HarperCollins, 1962.

Dyson, M. E. *Race Rules: Navigating the Color Line.* Reading, Mass.: Addison-Wesley, 1996.

Fine, M., and Weis, L. *The Unknown City: Lives of Poor and Working-Class Young Adults.* Boston: Beacon Press, 1998.

Fitzsimmons, S. *Distribution of Negro Population by County: Showing Each County with Five Hundred Negro Population,* Vol. 11. Washington, D.C.: U.S. Department of Commerce, Bureau of the Census, 1950.

Floyd, S. A. *The Power of Black Music: Interpreting Its History from Africa to the United States.* New York: Oxford University Press, 1995.

Fordham, S. "Ebonics as Guerilla Warfare." *Anthropology and Education*, 1999, *30*(3), 272-293.

Fordham, S., and Ogbu, J. U. "Black Students' School Success: Coping with the Burden of 'Acting White.' *Urban Review*, 1986, *18*(3), 176-206.

Franklin, J. H. *From Slavery to Freedom: A History of Negro Americans.* (3rd ed.) New York: Vintage Books, 1969.

Gannett, H. *Statistical Atlas of the United States Based on the Results of the Eleventh Census 1890.* Washington, D.C.: U.S. Government Printing Office, 1898.

Gee, J. P. *Social Linguistics and Literacies: Ideology in Discourses.* (2nd ed.) London: Taylor & Francis, 1996.

Gilroy, P. "Its a Family Affair." In G. Dent (ed.), *Black Popular Culture.* New York: New Press, 1998.

Giroux, H. A., and McLaren, P. *Between Borders: Pedagogy and the Politics of Cultural Studies.* New York: Routledge, 1994.

Guy, T. C. "Culturally Relevant Literacy Instruction for African American Adults: African American English (AAE) as an Instructional Resource for Teachers of African American Adults." In D. Ntiri (ed.), *Pedagogy for Adult Learners: Methods and Strategies,* Vol. 2: *Models for Adult and Lifelong Learning,* no. 2. Detroit: Office of Adult and Lifelong Research, Wayne State University, 1999.

Guy, T. C. "Culture Wars in Predominately Black, Urban, ABE Classrooms." *Cyril O. Houle Scholars in Adult and Continuing Education Program, Global Research Perspectives,* Vol. 3. Athens: University of Georgia, 2003.

Hacker, A. *Two Nations: Black and White, Separate, Hostile and Unequal.* New York: Scribner, 1992.

Haymes, S. N. *Race, Culture, and the City: A Pedagogy for Black Urban Struggle.* Albany: State University of New York Press, 1995.

Hounsel, W. "Chuck D. Speaks on Hip-Hop, Politics." *Asheville Global Report,* Mar. 2, 2003, p. 12.

Hughes, L. "The Best of Simple." In H.L. Gates and N. Y. McKay (eds.), *Norton Anthology of African American Literature.* New York: Norton, 1965.

Jeffries, J. "Toward a Redefinition of the Urban." In G. Dent (ed.), *Black Popular Culture.* New York: New Press, 1998.

Kellner, D. *Media Culture: Cultural Studies, Identity, and Politics Between the Modern and the Postmodern.* London: Routledge, 1995.

Kelly, N. "Political Economy of Black Music." *Black Renaissance/Renaissance Noire,* 1999, 2(2), 9–21.

Kerner Commission on Civil Disorders. *Report of the National Advisory Commission on Civil Disorders.* New York: Bantam, 1968.

Locke, A. (ed.). *The New Negro.* New York: A. C. Boni, 1925.

Lukes, S. *Emile Durkheim, His life and Work: A Historical and Critical Study.* London,: Allen Lane, 1973.

Massey, D. S., and Denton, N. A. *American Apartheid: Segregation and the Making of the Underclass.* Cambridge, Mass.: Harvard University Press, 1993.

McCarthy, C. *Sound Identities: Popular Music and the Cultural Politics of Education.* New York: Peter Lang, 1999.

McLaren, P. Gangsta Pedagogy and Ghettocentricity: "The Hip-Hop Nation and Ghettocentricity as Counterpublic Sphere." In C. McCarthy, G. Hudak, S. A. Allegretto, M. Shawn, and P. Saukko (eds.), *Sound Identities: Popular Music and the Cultural Politics of Education.* New York: Peter Lang, 1999.

Negre, J. S., and Bernet, J. T. *L'education en milieu urban: la ville educatrice.* Paris: United Nations Educational, Scientific, and Cultural Organization, 1993.

Patterson, O. *The Ordeal of Integration: Progress and Resentment in America's "Racial" Crisis.* Washington, D.C.: Civitas/Counterpoint, 1997.

Paul, D. G. "Rap and Orality: Critical Media Literacy, Pedagogy, and Cultural Synchronization." *Journal of Adolescent & Adult Literacy,* 2000, 44(3), 246–251.

Rodriguez, N. M. *Emptying the Contents of Whiteness: Toward an Understanding of the Relation Between Whiteness and Pedagogy.* New York: St. Martin's Press, 1998.

Rose, T. *Black Noise: Rap Music and Black Culture in Contemporary America.* Hanover, N.H.: Wesleyan University Press, 1994.

Sheared, V. Giving Voice: An Inclusive Model of Instruction—A Womanist Perspective. In E. Hayes and S.A.J. Colin (eds.), *Confronting Racism and Sexism in Adult and Continuing Education.* San Francisco: Jossey Bass, 1994.

Sheared, V. "Welfare Reform, Work, and Literacy: Issues of Gender, Class, and Race. Cyril O. Houle Scholars in Adult and Continuing Education Program, Global Research Perspectives, Vol. 1. Athens: University of Georgia, 2001.

Werner, C. H. *A Change Is Gonna Come: Music, Race and the Soul of America.* New York: Plume, 1998.

Williams, S. A. "Two Words on Music: Black Community." In G. Dent (ed.), Black Popular Culture. New York: New Press, 1998.

Wilson, W. J. *The Truly Disadvantaged: The Inner City, the Underclass, and Public Policy.* Chicago: University of Chicago Press, 1987.

Wright, R. *Native Son.* New York: Perennial Books, 2001. (Originally published 1940.)

TALMADGE C. GUY is associate professor in the Department of Adult Education, University of Georgia.

5

Responsive community programming assists urban learners in revitalizing their communities. This chapter examines two community-based organizations that are creating positive changes in local neighborhoods with collaborated strategies for the delivery of educational programming.

Learning to Rejuvenate Metropolitan Communities

E. Paulette Isaac, Martha Strittmatter Tempesta

Underlying the networks of social service programs that are targeted to benefit inner-city residents, the governmental funding priorities that are tied to political agendas, and the media emphasis on community deficits are assumptions of assigned helplessness and lack of sufficiency regarding inner-city minority populations. Assistance programs, frequently designed by well-intentioned agents external to the constituencies served, promise remedial results. Johnson and Farrell (1998) illustrate consequences of governmental policies intended to resolve inequities that instead create disparities in income varying by race and ethnicity, gender, and immigrant status. Such consequences are worsening as the twenty-first century begins.

Critical, then, are educational programs that produce lasting positive changes. Initiatives that offer urban learners opportunities to develop internal resources and produce local social capital result in long-term benefits of individual and community change for disadvantaged populations of the central city.

Urban revitalization challenges are constant and pervasive. Included are collaboration among local constituencies and external resources, public discourse between advocacy and political groups, quality education, crime reduction, adequate housing, employment, and neighborhood improvements contributing to quality of life. These are appropriate expectations of all citizens. Resolutions by community groups to overcome the challenges of poverty, galvanized by racism and inequality, are a considerable undertaking in which it is essential to engage local residents.

For significant social change to occur in America's inner cities, the people who live there must decide what their future is going to be, and they

NEW DIRECTIONS FOR ADULT AND CONTINUING EDUCATION, no. 101, Spring 2004 © Wiley Periodicals, Inc.

must be engaged in implementing social change (Etzioni, 1993; Highlander Research and Education Center, 2000; Kretzmann and McKnight, 1993; Krumholz and Clavel, 1994; Zielenbach, 1998). Wilson (1996), Cunningham (1993), and Brookfield (1987) encourage a vision to democratize America with programs that effectively combat the problems of urban society. Katz (1993) believes that to bring about resolution, those affected by the problems perpetuated by racism must be included in the discourse. This is significant because residents of inner-city communities "clearly understand the inner workings and contradictions of their world better than do middle-class politicians and academics" (p. 332).

Adult education practitioners, traditionally dedicated to processes of empowerment and democracy, are likely proponents to facilitate the articulation and comprehension of that hidden transcript, no matter how incongruous it might seem when positioned against what policymakers and grassroots organizers believe are the real needs of their constituencies (Horton and Freire, 1990). Thus, the first step toward liberation is when an individual understands his or her inhibitions, frustrations, and subjugations and takes action for change (Lindeman, 1961).

The worsening of urban conditions supports the allegation that questions the adequacy of local social capital and of local leadership capacity to guide the renewal of urban communities that are in transition or crisis (Johnson and Farrell, 1998; Katz, 1993; Putnam, 2000; Wilson, 1987, 1996, 1999). The human and social capital of grassroots organizations and social movements exemplify the potential for learning and leadership development. Community-based organizations have experienced success in developing leaders and providing educational programming, which in turn aid in the renewal of communities to provide residents with a quality of life in which economic, social, and educational needs are satisfied.

Community Programs

A community has often been defined as a group of people living together as a smaller social unit within a larger unit and having similar interests in common. Hence, for purposes of this discussion, a *community-based program* is defined as a program that operates or functions within the boundaries of where the population being served resides. Conversely, faith-based organizations (FBOs) are centered on a common set of strong moral beliefs, truths, and values around which members align with trust and confidence and to which the membership remains loyal and constant. It is important to note that unlike community-based programs, FBOs may or may not be composed only of local residents.

Community and faith-based institutions and organizations have often served as major conduits of change in urban communities. While many urban areas continue the struggles of revitalization, there are examples of creative, collaborative efforts by residents to transform themselves and their communities. In this chapter we examine two organizations—MICAH and Grace Hill Neighborhood Services—and their respective approaches to eradicating social ills and revitalizing communities. For the purposes of our discussion, we specifically examined one faith-based organization dedicated to transformation through social action, and a community-based organization with a focus on individual and community development. The program sites were in Milwaukee, Wisconsin, and St. Louis, Missouri, respectively.

Urban Milwaukee. Economically and residentially isolated by white flight to the suburbs, Milwaukee's inner-city population, predominately minority, gained little during the prosperous 1990s. The Milwaukee Urban League's *Annual Report* (2000) revealed the negatives, including un- and under-employment, poor health, substandard housing, and injustice. Emphasized were not only the obstacles in the path of African Americans but also the need for African Americans to accept some responsibility for their predicament. Levine (2000, p. 172), an economic development expert at the University of Wisconsin-Milwaukee, emphasized, "Black Milwaukee remains the most economically disadvantaged big city African-American community in the country." The growth of the city's Hispanic community makes it imperative that blacks and Latinos start thinking about developing a "common vision focused on their well-being" (p. 172). Accordingly, the consensus appears to be that the social problems and the resources for change coexist.

MICAH. The Milwaukee Innercity Congregations Allied for Hope (MICAH) is a collaboration of faith-based communities committed to expressing their faith beliefs in actions for social justice in the urban arena. Within the coalitional structure of MICAH, individuals take action, supported by a belief in their personal and collective power to "free themselves" (Freire, 1985). An overarching objective of the coalition is the actualization of a new culture created from an egalitarian vision in which justice and equity are embraced as modes of behavior for the entire membership. Organized in faith communities, religious coalitions express much more than faith. They frequently offer vehicles of influence for those with social, political, and economic concerns. Hence, organizing among churches is a strategy for capitalizing on the existing assets in the inner city.

Holding fast to a firm resolution to accept no government funding, MICAH is a 501(c)3 organization supported by grants and public and private contributions. There are three full-time staff members—an executive director, a community organizer, and an office administrator. The Mott Foundation, Catholic Charities, and the Nonprofit Management Fund were among the funders in 2002–2003. Throughout the year, twenty leaders participated in an intensive week-long residential training program provided by the Gamaliel Foundation. A track in Spanish was also available. Approximately four hundred leaders participated in local training workshops.

MICAH has addressed a number of issues. For example, it has advocated treatment instead of prison for first-time, nonviolent criminal convictions. It has challenged the razing of a minority residential area and the demolition of the Park East Freeway to expose twenty-six acres of prime real estate for development. In addition, MICAH has demanded quality education for all Milwaukee public school students. Furthermore, through its labor committee, a job-creation campaign of planned public work has been initiated to benefit minority job seekers in certain areas of Milwaukee.

Significant to the membership is the inclusive climate of the coalition organized among inner-city congregations. Most significant are the ecumenical and multicultural characteristics of this coalition. The attractiveness of that criterion for urban revitalization is that nearly every community has faith-based foundations and meetings in worship places, churches, temples, and shrines that draw in people. Among these groups, MICAH organizes people and money to develop a constituency with power.

In addition to MICAH's multiracial and ecumenical composition there is a wide range in the social strata of its member churches. Included among the roster are suburban congregations, with one having an all-white, middle-class membership. Although tension around preserving inner-city control of MICAH's agenda results from the alliance, there is agreement on the notion that metropolitan politics and issues traverse the boundaries. Future resolutions of "metropolitics" mandate the collaboration between suburban and inner-city residents. At a recent annual fundraising banquet, the members of Bayshore Lutheran Church in Whitefish Bay, an upper middle-class suburban area, in partnership with Hephatha, a developing inner-city congregation, shared a table to hear keynote speaker Crystal Kuykendall, an African American, address common concerns for youth.

Capacity Building with Collaborated Leadership Learning. The expansion of social capital via leadership learning among the faith-based membership of this social justice movement reveals that faith values energize the passion of the participants and subsequently guide the direction of their work (Tempesta, 2001). The faith perspective is a discriminating factor that influences individuals, often with previous leadership experience, to align their abilities with the social justice movement coalition. Accessible within the context of the coalition and among the members, spiritual beliefs enrich the leaders and the work. The coalition provides a community in which the leaders have the opportunity to explore new ideas and develop new ways of thinking about how the world works (or ought to work). Activities, meetings, and the like offer the coalition's constituency the opportunity to develop relationships and become acquainted with one another beyond the tasks of social justice. Incidental learning advances the quality of human relationships far more effectively than an out-of-context diversity workshop ever could.

Collaboration with other faith-based organizations increases the volume and capacity of learning and leadership opportunities. Engagement outside the boundaries of local membership offers expanded opportunities to learn from one another, increases the participants' sphere of influence, and produces impressive numbers of people for public actions, positioning the organization to exercise political power. A shortage of material resources within the inner-city environment makes a compelling case for collaboration and is an instinctive choice for learning and action among the constituency.

Instructional Techniques. Within MICAH, the leaders experience a learning laboratory in which to gain knowledge, develop skills, test the applications in active community work, evaluate the results, and continue their pursuit of knowledge (Bandura, 1986; Cunningham and Curry, 1997; Galbraith and Cohen, 1995). Experiences have included a week-long workshop and periodic reinforcement of principles at meetings and gatherings, accompanied by unlimited opportunities to assume leadership and practice leadership skills. The learning in this inclusive, multicultural collaboration of the learners has been experiential, intentional, and incidental.

The learners have been as diverse as the learning and motivations for participation. As Tempesta (2001) indicates in her extensive examination of MICAH, the top leaders represent a variety of religious ideologies. Included are male and female African American, Hispanic, Latino, and White leaders ranging from ages twenty-seven to sixty. Educationally they consist of high school graduates as well as associate's and bachelor's degree recipients, and one individual with a doctoral degree. Hence, there are some commonalities among the instructional techniques to which they were exposed prior to their participation in MICAH.

A consistent format for meetings and gatherings establishes a structure for learning and leadership development. Meetings are conducted with an agenda and follow a format that includes a stated purpose (an objective) and prayer (reinforcing the organization's values), and conclude with evaluation and debriefing processes.

Within the learning environment, experienced and potential leaders intersect to collaborate for social justice. Structure is evident while informality prevails. Fostered among the community of activists, relationships reinforce the tenets of the coalition, agitation incites greater accomplishments, and partnerships accomplish the social justice goals, unattainable without the power of organized people and money. The importance of the learning context within which the MICAH leaders have shared learning experiences is revealed by the various occasions of this learning:

- Active engagement, with a focus on problematic issues
- "Communion" within the community of learners
- Acquiring new information or knowledge
- Modeling or mentoring among the leaders
- Reflection on events, circumstances, leadership, and so on

Creating the contextual aspects of the learning environment are the roles, stages of development, learning processes, and learning opportunities accessible at the various sites constituting the physical learning environment. They are essentially faith-based sites where planning meetings or gatherings take place, but they include community sites, the Gamaliel Foundation training site, and wherever two or more coalition members are in communion. Within the learning experiences, the leaders are in relation to one another, and the safety net of support is made available to provide a sense of security with allies. The encouraging words and environment extend leadership development at every opportunity where experimentation occurs.

Engaged within the coalition to create greater awareness of self and others is the tactic of agitation. Appreciating the role of self-interest is essential for comprehending the movement's strategies and its tactics used to agitate people. Employed in the larger contexts of society, the tactics are engaged to create change for social justice (Bowers, Ochs, and Jensen, 1993). MICAH's leaders participate in one another's development with agitations and challenges. Among the coalition's members and leaders, recipients consider agitations to be expressions of care and consideration. Tailored to the recipients, agitations are designed for particular circumstances. Some members can be moved with a softly spoken word, others require a nudge, and some need a push or, for the most resistant, a hard shove delivered with integrity.

Urban St. Louis. St. Louis is the largest metropolitan area in the state of Missouri. It ranks fourth among the most segregated cities in the United States (Freeman, 2002). Once composed of a predominately white population, it is now 52.7 percent African American and 44.6 percent white (Office of Social and Economic Data Analysis, 2003). In addition, between 1990 and 2000, there was a 12.2 percent decrease in the population (U.S. Census Bureau, 2003). As in other inner cities, St. Louis has experienced a decaying of sorts. Many dilapidated buildings line the streets, crime rates have risen, and businesses have relocated to the suburbs. This deterioration has been coupled with alarming statistics. Between 1980 and 1990 there was a 7.9 percent decrease in the number of individuals with a high school diploma. The city of St. Louis's 2002 dropout rate for grades 9 through 12 (7.8 percent) was more than double that for the entire state of Missouri (3.8 percent) (Missouri Department of Elementary and Secondary Education, 2003). The adult unemployment rate in 1999 was 7.8 percent (Office of Social and Economic Data Analysis, 2001). Such grim statistics strongly indicate a need for adult education interventions and programs.

Grace Hill Neighborhood Services. In St. Louis, Grace Hill Neighborhood Services (Grace Hill) has been successful in affecting individual and community change for urban residents for nearly one hundred years. This nonprofit, community-based agency initially began as a settlement house. Its mission includes working for social change within society to foster great support and understanding of the disadvantaged; working in disadvantaged neighborhoods creating strong, healthy communities; and providing direct services in a cost-efficient manner (*Grace Hill Mission Statement,* 2002).

Thus, Grace Hill continues to be committed not only to "adapting programs and services in response to the changing needs of people but also to challenging the social and economic condition that created those needs" (Grace Hill Neighborhood Services, 2000, p. 2).

Similarly to other nonprofit agencies, Grace Hill receives funding from a variety of areas, including public and private sources. It receives annual funding from the United Way. It has also received funding from the National Park Service, Missouri Children's Trust Fund, the Division of Family Services, and the Environmental Protection Agency. Funding is pursued based on identified needs of the community.

Capacity Building Through Grace Hill Neighborhood College. Grace Hill Neighborhood College (GHNC) exemplifies Grace Hill's logo, "Neighbors Helping Neighbors." The 1982 cutbacks in federal funding served as the impetus for the creation of GHNC (Grace Hill Neighborhood Services, 2000). Initially relying on professionals to provide services for residents, GHNC soon realized its best resources for addressing issues were the residents themselves.

GHNC offers classes at different sites throughout St. Louis. Each site employs a center coordinator and resident trainer. The coordinator's responsibilities include, among other things, directing the recruiting and screening of neighbors (residents), ensuring integration of all programs at assigned sites and conducting door-to-door outreach. The resident trainer prepares training schedules for future classes, arranges for guest speakers, and follows up with trainees (students) on field assignments. Approximately ten volunteers, depending on the number of courses taught, assist the coordinator and resident trainer.

One of the unique aspects of GHNC is that residents teach and learn from one another, with decisions regarding course offerings being made by the residents. In many respects, the Neighborhood College is similar to a formal college. Although open to the general public, residents within Grace Hill's service areas receive priority for admittance to courses. Courses are free and residents receive a small stipend for course completion, which can be used to defray expenses such as transportation, child care, utilities, or household supplies.

While a college degree, or even any formal college experience, is not a requisite for teaching a course at GHNC, residents who teach must complete a predetermined number of GHNC courses before they can teach their fellow residents. As this requirement suggests, resident trainers' formal educational backgrounds can vary. Residents choose to teach for diverse reasons. Some are motivated to teach for financial purposes, as instructors receive a small stipend. Others feel they possess the necessary leadership skills to teach a course. Still others have completed a particular course and feel they have gained the self-confidence they need to educate others.

More than fifty courses are offered on aging, business and employment, child care and parenting, and wellness and community health. Older adults in the community are trained to provide assistance to other older adults, including information and referral services. Furthermore, they learn record keeping and respite care. Students at GHNC are given the opportunity to obtain information on how to start and manage a business and on how to find career opportunities. Under the auspices of child care and parenting courses, students learn how to provide a safe and healthy environment for children, child-rearing skills, and aspects of a normal pregnancy. Residents can also learn about providing child care services in their homes. In addition, courses are taught on asthma, nutrition, the community environment, stress management, and smoking cessation. Through Grace Hill, more than two hundred residents have been placed in jobs. Armed with knowledge gained from the college, and more specifically from their fellow residents, participants can make positive changes in their lives and communities. The college can provide them with a way to reconnect with mainstream America. Many participants have moved from the welfare rolls by obtaining full-time employment. A single mother with an asthmatic child took an asthma class, eventually became a paid coordinator for Grace Hill, and subsequently took a position with a social service agency in St. Louis. The college continues to survive to serve the neighborhood constituency.

Instructional Techniques. Grace Hill Neighborhood College uses a variety of instructional techniques. Many classes consist of classroom and field-work hours. However, some classes, like Co-CARE III, a parenting class, incorporate skill building, role-playing, and discussion as instructional techniques. Additional techniques include hands-on training. To illustrate, adults enrolled in a nutrition course visit a grocery store and plan and prepare a nutritional meal. With a focus on the individual and the community, different techniques are used to aid urban adult learners in examining a plethora of topics and issues that can have positive effects in their homes and neighborhoods.

Conclusion

Characterizing these two illustrations of urban community revitalization are strict devotion to a social change agenda, initiated and articulated by the grassroots citizenry, with an emphasis on self-sufficiency and capacity building among the local constituency. MICAH and Grace Hill dispel the notion that inner-city residents are helpless and have nothing of value to contribute to the development of their communities. Furthermore, the activities and subsequent experiences facilitated by these two organizations are meaningful and provide learning opportunities because they are postured as expressions of strong values and personal commitment. They are expressions of strongly held beliefs about how the world ought to work.

As in any educational setting, no one method can best serve all learners. However, these two models disclose a variety of overarching strategies and instructional techniques. None could or should be replicated intact. The model used by MICAH is the effort to develop leaders from the community to aggressively pursue positive social change. Grace Hill suggests a self-help strategy in which members of the community teach one another. A commonality of both organizations is their investment in the inner-city residents in the hope that they will become active learning leaders effecting change in their local communities.

The programmatic efforts by MICAH and Grace Hill are offered as models for emulation or adaptation to enhance learning and effect community change. They are only two examples of urban revitalization efforts. Community-based programs can not only meet the educational needs of adult learners, the only reliable and consistent resource within the community, but also empower them to effect change in their communities. For some adults who have been outside of mainstream society for years, participation in programs that aid in the revitalization of their community provides the positive experience necessary for their personal development, attainment of employment, or participation in formal technical training or education. As models of education for urban residents, MICAH and Grace Hill demonstrate that, with involvement from the residents themselves, effective change can occur in our urban communities.

References

Bandura, A. *Social Foundations of Thought and Action: A Social Cognitive Theory.* Englewood Cliffs, N.J.: Prentice Hall, 1986.

Bowers, J. W., Ochs, D. J., and Jensen, R. J. *The Rhetoric of Agitation and Control.* (2nd ed.) Prospect Heights, Ill.: Waveland Press, 1993.

Brookfield, S. *Developing Critical Thinkers.* San Francisco: Jossey-Bass, 1987.

Cunningham. P. "Let's Get Real: A Critical Look at the Practice of Adult Education." *Journal of Adult Education,* 1993, 22(1), 3–5.

Cunningham, P., and Curry, R. "Learning Within a Social Movement: The Chicago African-American Experiences." *Adult Education Research Conference Proceedings.* [http://www.edu.ubs.ca/edst/aerc], 1997.

Etzioni, A. *The Spirit of Community: The Reinvention of American Society.* New York: Simon & Schuster, 1993.

Freeman, G. "St. Louis Is Among Most-Segregated Cities." *St. Louis Post-Dispatch,* Dec. 1, 2002, p. G3.

Freire, P. *The Politics of Education: Culture, Power and Liberation.* Westport, Conn.: Bergin & Garvey, 1985.

Galbraith, M. W., and Cohen, H. H. (eds.). *Mentoring: New Strategies and Challenges.* New Directions for Adult and Continuing Education, no. 66. San Francisco: Jossey-Bass, 1995.

Grace Hill Mission Statement. St. Louis, Mo.: Grace Hill Settlement House [http://www.gracehill.org], retrieved Oct. 30, 2002.

Grace Hill Neighborhood Services. *Neighborhood College Catalogue 2000–2001.* St. Louis, Mo.: Grace Hill Settlement House, 2000.

Grace Hill Settlement House. *MORE: Member Organized Resource Exchange—A Guide to Replication.* St. Louis, Mo.: Grace Hill Settlement House, 2000.

Highlander Research and Education Center. "Welcome to Highlander…" [http://www.hrec.org], retrieved May 6, 2000.

Horton, M., and Freire, P. *We Make the Road by Walking.* Philadelphia: Temple University Press, 1990.

Johnson, J., and Farrell, W. "Growing Income Inequality in American Society: A Political Economy Perspective." In J. Auerbach and R. Belous (eds.), *The Inequality Paradox: Growth of Income Disparity.* Washington, D.C.: National Policy Administration, 1998.

Katz, M. B. *The Underclass Debate: Views from History.* Princeton, N.J.: Princeton University Press, 1993.

Kretzmann, J. P., and McKnight, J. L. *Building Communities from the Inside Out: A Path Toward Finding and Mobilizing a Community's Assets.* Chicago: Asset-Based Community Development Institute, 1993.

Krumholz, N., and Clavel, P. *Reinventing Cities: Equity Planners Tell Their Stories.* Philadelphia: Temple University Press, 1994.

Levine, M. "The Economic State of Black Milwaukee." In S. Battle and R. Hornung (eds.), *The State of Black Milwaukee.* Milwaukee: Milwaukee Urban League, 2000.

Lindeman, E. C. *The Meaning of Adult Education.* New York: New Republic, 1961. (Originally published 1926.)

Milwaukee Urban League. *Annual Report.* Milwaukee, Minn.: Milwaukee Urban League, 2000.

Missouri Department of Elementary and Secondary Education. "Annual Dropout Rate 1999-2003 as a Percent of Total Enrollment" (table) [http://www.dese.state.mo.us/schooldata/four/115115/dropnone.html], retrieved Apr. 30, 2003.

Office of Social and Economic Data Analysis. *Missouri County Fact Sheets.* [http://www.oseda.missouri.edu/countypage], retrieved Apr. 30, 2003.

Putnam, R. *Bowling Alone.* New York: Simon & Schuster, 2000.

Tempesta, M. S. "A Phenomenological Study of Learning Experiences Contributing to Leadership Capacity in Urban Faith-Based Communities. Doctoral dissertation, University of Wisconsin, Milwaukee, 2001. *Dissertation Abstracts International* A 62/11, P3660.

U.S. Census Bureau. State and County QuickFacts: St. Louis City, Missouri. [http://quickfacts.census.gov/qfd/states/29/29510.html], retrieved Apr. 18, 2003.

Wilson, W. *The Truly Disadvantaged: The Inner City, the Underclass, and Public Policy.* Chicago: University of Chicago Press, 1987.

Wilson, W. *When Work Disappears.* New York: Knopf, 1996.

Wilson, W. *The Bridge over the Racial Divide.* Berkeley: University of California Press, 1999.

Zielenbach, S. "The Art of Revitalization: Improving Conditions in Distressed Inner-City Neighborhoods." Doctoral dissertation, Northwestern University, 1998. *Dissertation Abstracts International* 59:05, AAC9832724.

E. PAULETTE ISAAC is assistant professor of adult education at the University of Missouri-St. Louis.

MARTHA STRITTMATTER TEMPESTA is director of the Center for New Learning at the University of Wisconsin-Oshkosh.

6

The digital divide is leaving millions disenfranchised from the opportunity to use technology to change their lives and to participate fully in democracy, in their own communities, and in today's job market.

Narrowing the Digital Divide in Low-Income, Urban Communities

Daniel T. Norris, Simone Conceição

Information technology seems uniquely suited to solve many adult education concerns. It is infinitely adaptable to the many environments in which adults live and work and to the many learning styles that adults exhibit. It is also available on demand for that moment when time and informational need meet to solve a pressing problem. However, adaptability and timely presence are not the only factors favoring technology in adult education, especially within an urban setting. In fact, these productive and useful attributes of technology are available to less than 9 percent of the world's population (Levine, 2002; U.S. Census Bureau, 2002). While this figure includes rural, urban, developed, and undeveloped peoples and countries, it is indicative of the lopsided distribution between those who have access to technology and those who do not.

One good example of information technology that has become an omnipresent part of our personal and business activities is the computer. However, as computer interconnectivity becomes increasingly important to personal economic and social success, many people in the central cities and isolated rural areas are failing to acquire the new technology as rapidly as their more affluent neighbors (U.S. Congress, 2001). This situation is leaving millions disenfranchised from the opportunity to use technology to change their lives and contribute to their communities. At stake is whether individuals are able to participate fully in democracy, in their own communities, and in today's job market.

Current research indicates a relationship between possessing computer skills and attaining or maintaining employment (Groneman, 2000). Duranton (2002, p. 1) states that "technology and the way it has evolved are viewed by many as a very likely causal factor for this widespread rise in [wage] inequalities." Such foreboding makes evident the value of computer access and skills. Access to computers has been decidedly unequal, however. According to U.S. Census data ranging from 1990 to 2000, the typical computer user in the United States is white, between the ages of twenty-five and forty-four, college educated, and married with an annual household income above $75,000 (Kominski, 1992; Newburger, 2001). The Internet is relatively new on the scene, but usage statistics from 1997 and 2000 indicate a similar demographic (Newburger, 1997, 2001).

Slowly, however, these demographics are changing, at least in the United States. What this statistical snapshot does not reveal is that within the last ten years, minorities have been increasingly acquiring computers and using the Internet (Newburger, 1997, 2001; Kominski, 1992). The U.S. Department of Commerce reports a narrowing of technological inequality in America (Mineta, 2000). The report points out that there are more computers in the United States than in the rest of the world combined. North Americans also dominate Internet use, with 41 percent of the global online population living in the United States and Canada (Digital Divide Network, 2002). While the gap may be narrowing across the United States as a whole, there is still a divide. And nowhere is the gap wider than in the urban centers of the major U.S. cities.

Enthusiasts for the prospects of the computer and the Internet to equalize opportunity have strongly fastened these technologies to the bulwark of adult education. Yet, with the seemingly boundless growth of information technology, our urban centers are not experiencing a narrowing of the gap. In fact, the gap is widening between those who have access to information technology and those who do not (Graham, 2001; Hoffman and Novak, 1998). This gap is commonly referred to as the digital divide.

This chapter addresses the digital divide and its consequences for urban adult education. The contexts of information technology, race, and culture are identified to help the reader comprehend some of the factors that affect the digital divide in adult education. Then the obstacles to access and use of information technology and opportunities to further narrow the digital divide in urban communities are presented.

Context of Information Technology, Race, and Culture in the Digital Divide

The term information technology includes all forms of technologies used to create, store, exchange, and use information in different formats (data, voice, video, still images, multimedia presentations, and so on). Information technology is a combination of many technologies that provide access to formal, nonformal, and informal education (Coombs, Prosser, and Ahmed, 1973). Formal education involves learning in educational institutions that may allow the learner to gain a degree or certification (credit or noncredit, long-term or short-term). Nonformal education consists of planned activities organized by learning centers, churches, or voluntary associations. Informal education comprises "experiences of everyday living from which [individuals] learn something" (Merriam and Caffarella, 1999, p. 22). Informal learning may involve individuals searching the Internet for the sake of their own learning, using chat rooms to collaborate with other people, using an online database to search for a family tree, and so on.

The faceless nature of computerized communication technology allows relatively unbiased access regardless of gender, disability, creed, race, or culture. However, race and culture might bias how the Internet is used. To comprehend how race and culture might influence the application of the Internet, or computer technology in general, an understanding of how race and culture are defined is needed. The concepts of race and culture are closely related. The U.S. Census Bureau (1995) defines race as individual self-identification by people according to the race or races with which they most closely identify. Culture too is considered a group with which an individual identifies (Richardson, Spears, and Richards, 1972). Samovar and Porter (1972) refer to culture as the cumulative deposit of knowledge, experience, beliefs, values, attitudes, meanings, hierarchies, religion, notions of time, roles, spatial relations, concepts of the universe, and material objects and possessions acquired by a group of people in the course of generations through individual and group striving. In this chapter, culture refers to how a particular race may perceive information technology due to their shared behavioral heritage. The term race is used here as a convenient dividing line for the categories of the digital divide and implies an associated culture.

Factors Affecting Access to and Usage of Information Technology

There are three factors relevant to the digital divide in adult education: urban location, culture, and literacy. The urban location factor is space related. The culture factor is related to cultural heritage and, as promoted here, is an underconsidered component of the digital divide in urban environments. The literacy factor is directly connected to access and use of information technologies. Literacy is more than reading ability and developing a set of computer skills (that is, keyboarding, creating and using spreadsheets, word processing, using a database, and so on). Within the digital divide, the term literacy has gone beyond the commonly used definition: "using printed and written information to function in society, to achieve one's goals, and to develop one's knowledge and potential" (National Center for Education Statistics, 2003). When paired with the word computer, the word literacy is defined by Webster's II New College Dictionary (1999) as "the ability to use a computer and its software to accomplish practical tasks." As used in this chapter, literacy also includes a level of understanding of how computer operation skills interact and interchange regardless of application. Like income and culture, literacy affects urban adult participation in formal, nonformal, and informal adult education activities.

Urban Location Factor. Access to information technology for central city citizens amounts to only 37.7 percent compared to 38.9 percent for rural areas and 42.3 percent for urban areas in general. Central cities house disproportionately more poor people than anywhere else in the nation (Proctor and Dalaker, 2002). According to the U.S. Department of Commerce (1998), Internet access in central cities is very low; only 22.8 percent of female-headed households have Internet access compared to 51 percent of households nationally. Because more than half of all African Americans and Hispanics live in central cities (Bullard, Johnson, and Torres, 2000), it is within the central city that the digital divide takes on more racial overtones.

Poverty is not the only issue when considering urban adults' barriers to information technologies. Hoffman, Novak, and Schlosser (2000, p. 5) indicate that "while income explains race differences in home computer ownership, Whites are still more likely to own a home computer than African Americans at all income levels." This fact hints that culture, which may be attached to race, might also be a factor in the digital divide, because U.S. Census Bureau (2000) data indicate that income and education alone cannot explain usage differences between races. Also, the U.S. Census data do not offer Internet usage statistics specific to urban communities. Central-city computer and Internet usage statistics are few and far between, presumably because of the lack of access to the technology. However, racially specific Internet usage patterns can be discerned by looking at national statistics as a whole.

For example, Hispanics represent the fastest growing ethnic group in America; they currently number more than thirty-five million, which is 12.5 percent of the total U.S. population (U.S. Census Bureau, 2000). According to Spooner and Rainie's (2001) study, 50 percent of Hispanics who are eighteen and older (more than twenty-one million) have used the Internet; half of these are accessing the Internet from household computers. Asian Americans, however, are the most connected of any race in the United States relative to the size of their population. Seventy-five percent of English-speaking Asian-American adults have used the Internet, with approximately 70 percent using the Internet daily (Spooner, 2001), and 56 percent have Internet access at home (U.S. Census Bureau, 2000). White Americans, at 46.1 percent, are second only to Asian Americans in home Internet use. African Americans match Hispanics in home Internet access and make up only 23.6 percent of all Americans with Internet access in the home (U.S. Census Bureau, 2000).

In summary, these statistics indicate that Asian American usage of Internet technology is highest, followed by white Americans. African Americans and Hispanics share the trailing edge of home use of the Internet.

However, according to Spooner (2001), Hispanic Internet use is on the rise. This claim is supported by U.S. Census data (2000) indicating Hispanic households with computers have a 1 percent edge over African American households. While it can be said that these home Internet usage statistics relate strongly to income and education (Coley, Cradler, and Engel, 1997), research has shown that culture can be an influencing factor in explaining the lack of uniformity in these numbers (Hoffman and Novak, 1998).

Culture Factor. According to Haymes (1995), culture is learned, and it affects how one approaches or interprets the world, especially when one's culture is not the dominant culture. How one's culture relates to the dominant culture, and vice versa, is key when considering how an individual may perceive information technology and its use in formal, informal, or nonformal educational contexts. To offer an example of this phenomena, marketing and economic research indicates that some racial groups "have participated in greater measure in entertainment-oriented technologies rather than in information-oriented technologies" (Hoffman, Novak, and Venkatesh, 1997, p. 4).

In an attempt to explain this phenomenon, Hoffman, Novak, and Venkatesh (1997) propose that because some minorities have been relegated to a subset of the dominant white culture, they have sought to make their mark in areas not so dominated by whites. Additionally, they hypothesize that because the computer itself has "arisen from the white, male culture," the use of it may threaten to deconstruct cultural integrity (p. 4).

Contrary to Hoffman, Novak, and Venkatesh (1997), Kolko, Nakamura, and Rodman (2000) suggest that it is not one's position within the dominant culture that affects information technology usage; rather, it is the level of importance at which a given culture perceives the act of gathering information and the importance given to education that affect technology choices. This supposition is supported by U.S. Census Bureau (2000) data depicting online information retrieval patterns that are divided along racial lines. Thirty-four percent of Asian American adult users get the daily news online compared with only 20 percent of Hispanic adults and 15 percent of African American adults (Spooner and Rainie, 2001), compared to 61 percent of online whites who have ever used the Internet to get news (Rainie and Packel, 2001). These statistics align strongly with the Internet home usage statistics presented earlier but do not necessarily follow economic status levels.

Literacy Factor. One factor that is directly linked to adult education is literacy, because in order for individuals to use information technologies, they must have reached a basic literacy level. Literacy involves not only being able to read in the language of the dominant culture, but also being able to read in the language of one's own culture. Also, using information technology to acquire knowledge requires new reading skills and computer savvy (National Adult Literacy Database, 2000). For example, a computer user needs to know how to navigate and make meaning of nonlinear text, as well as how to search, find, authenticate, and utilize various types of documents in a digital environment (Rocap, 2002). Consequently, digital literacy and language literacy are significant issues affecting the learning experience of an adult.

The Children's Partnership, a national nonprofit, nonpartisan organization that does research and advocates on behalf of underserved youth conducted a survey of Internet content and found that at least 20 percent of American adults are likely to be underserved because of Internet content related to literacy, language, or content relevance (Lazarus and Mora, 2000). About 87 percent of Internet content is in English and written at standard or higher literacy levels, making 22 percent of the older U.S. population unable to benefit from the resources available on the Internet. According to Lazarus and Mora (2000, p. 7), "at least 32 million Americans speak a language other than English as their primary language." They further report that what adults want is practical information focusing on local community programs, jobs, housing opportunities, education, events, and information that is written in a helpful and useful manner. But helpful and useful information would mean that content would have to be written at a literacy level that even a child might understand.

Community information must be relevant to the users and to the community to which they belong. One example of irrelevant material that makes the Web unapproachable, irrelevant, or unappealing to Hispanics in the United States is that most Spanish-language sites deal with topics that are significant to people in Latin America or Spain and not with opportunities or programs in communities in the United States (Lazarus and Mora, 2000). If the World Wide Web is to be used to disseminate information or educate adults, it must also address the fact that Hispanics make up the largest foreign-born minority group in the United States (Spooner, 2001). A medium as potent as the Internet has a responsibility to disseminate information to everyone.

Obstacles to Access and Use of Information Technology in Urban Communities

Adults in the central city face life issues similar to those of everyone else; however, they experience more obstacles to resources than do adults in suburban areas and in more affluent sections of a city (Danziger, 1999; De Haymes, Kilty, and Segal, 2000). Lack of money; time; access to technology, information, and resources; skills in the use of information technologies; and literacy are considered barriers in urban adult life (Coley, Cradler, and Engel, 1997; Danziger, 1999; Mineta, 2000; Merriam and Caffarella, 1999). Thus, the significance of supporting adults in low-income urban communities is critical for narrowing the digital divide.

While computer prices continue to drop, the price of a computer with monitor, speakers, software, and a printer can be as much as 10 to

15 percent of a poverty level income for a family of four. It takes time to learn the skills necessary to operate a computer and connect it to the Internet. More and more information is disseminated through the Internet. However, lack of culturally diverse Internet content and lack of local information about community assets have a direct effect on the use of information technology by certain racial or ethnic groups in urban communities (Lazarus and Mora, 2000; Gilster, 1997).

As an adult education instructional tool, information technology has the potential to bring education and life-changing information to adults. It can offer access to educational programs that grant diplomas and certifications. Urban adults can connect to the Internet to do school- or employment-related work at home while tending to child care. When connected to information, adults may widen their community perspective, thereby increasing opportunities for expression, self-fulfillment, and participation in citizenship.

Though information technology can be a tool for education and growth for central-city citizens, the only way it will make a difference is if it is used effectively to respond to the needs of individuals and their communities. Educators of adults can play a role in connecting urban adults to formal, nonformal, and informal education through information technologies by being aware of available programs and funding opportunities that can help eliminate the barriers related to access and usage.

Opportunities to Narrow the Digital Divide

A number of governmental and nongovernmental organizations are attempting to provide access to technology and training opportunities for underserved communities. These organizations focus on building community technology infrastructure, providing training and access to technology, creating links to relevant resources on the Web, and setting up portals (that is, clearinghouses of resources) on issues related to urban education and equity.

Technology Opportunities Program. Under the leadership of the U.S. Commerce Department's National Telecommunications and Information Administration, the Technology Opportunities Program (TOP) has awarded grants to nonprofit organizations and to state and local governments in the United States and Puerto Rico. The purpose of the TOP grants is to "extend the benefits of advanced telecommunications technologies to underserved communities and neighborhoods" (Wiburg and Butler, 2002, p. 7). This program provides communities with seed money, matched by additional public and private investment (Harris and Associates, 2002). Information about this program can be found at http://www.ntia.doc.gov/top.

Digital Promise Project. The Digital Promise Project is a proposal to create an educational trust fund (Digital Opportunity Investment Trust, or DO IT) designed to help transform education, training, and lifelong learning in the twenty-first century. This educational trust fund—a nonprofit, non-governmental agency—would be financed by revenue from auctions of unused, publicly owned telecommunications band-width spectrum, as mandated by Congress. The fund would be used to develop educational programs in schools, universities, libraries, and museums and to support research and development of new educational models and prototypes. Information about DO IT can be found at http://www.digitalpromise.org.

Community Technology Centers. The Community Technology Centers (CTCs) is a nonprofit membership organization in the United States with more than seven hundred independent community technology centers (Zgoda, 2002; Wiburg and Butler, 2002). These centers provide free or low-cost access to computers, computer-related technology, and user support. They are being erected in cities all over the United States (Yu, 2002) and provide the connection so desperately needed in the central city. The CTCs provide access to youth, adults, and seniors, serve as technical assistance providers to other nonprofits, and provide job training, counseling, or placement (Zgoda, 2002).

The creation of technology centers within urban communities in the United States is one avenue of access with many success stories. One example of a CTC is the Break Away Technologies community center initiative in South Central Los Angeles. This community center offers after-school and weekend programs for central city K-12 children, youth, and adults. One of their activities for adults is a CyberSeniors program. Seniors participate in the program to gain high-tech entrepreneurial skills. In addition, they serve as mentors to neighborhood youth. One of the goals of the Break Away center is to provide community-based and managed open access, education, training, and support centers to underserved young adults so they can "gain access to and develop competencies in using, building and maintaining computer and network technologies, use computers and the Internet for other learning activities and engage in web page development, multimedia, animation and graphic design courses, as well as develop work readiness and preparation skills" (Wiburg and Butler, 2002, p. 7).

Many CTCs have incorporated classes and training into their services, as well as free-form public access hours (Zgoda, 2002). This development is significant to educators of urban adults in that there appears to be a grassroots demand for training and education even if it is coming at the expense of offering noneducational information technology services to the community as a whole. Information about the CTCs can be found at http://www.ctcnet.org.

Links to Resources on the Web. Some organizations have focused their efforts on building relevant resources on the Web that address issues of inequity. One innovative project that offers home access to technology resources is Quepasa.com (http://www.quepasa.com), which provides access to news and information in English and Spanish to the Hispanic population in the United States. It also offers links to resources, chat rooms, and a search engine (Ingle, 2002). Another example of a Web resource is the Borderland Encyclopedia (http://www.utep.edu/border), which is a "digital repository of educational resources on the U.S./Mexico," developed by faculty and students at the University of Texas El Paso (Ingle, 2002, p. 82).

A Web site that has been developed to create awareness about issues related to the digital divide is http://LaBrechaDigital.org (the Digital Divide). This Web site makes available the names of individuals who are "instrumental in defining technology within the context of multicultural population groups and provides information on diverse learning styles, cultural background, and lifestyle conditions that interact with media content and educational information across America's changing demography" (Ingle, 2002, p. 83).

Conexiones Latinas is an organization that is trying to bridge the Spanish language divide by providing information on community resources in English and Spanish. Its Web site (http://www.conexioneslatinas.org) offers information and links specific to the local Hispanic community and is an excellent example of focusing Internet power on local issues.

Following is a list of a variety of links that attempt to connect specific ethnic groups with pertinent practical information. The list is by no means complete and is offered solely to help illustrate how the Web can be used as a community building tool.

African American Web Connection	http://www.aawc.com/aawc0.html
African American Resources from the Chico High School Library	http://dewey.chs.chico.k12.ca.us/afri.html
Jananoir: A Selected Guide to African American Resources on the Internet	http://www.javanoir.net/guide
Internet Resources on Asian Americans	http://newton.uor.edu/Departments&Programs/AsianStudiesDept/asianam.html
Asian American Cybernauts	http://www.janet.org/~ebihara/wataru_aacyber.html
Asian American Studies Page at the University of California, Santa Barbara Library	http://www.library.ucsb.edu/subj/asian-am.html

Portals. The term portal refers to an interactive and personalized clearinghouse that provides access to a variety of resources and tools. Rather than housing information itself, it houses pointers and documentation about resources and presents information in an organized way to a user, much like a report generator does for a database. In this case the database is the Web itself, as filtered by the portal's editors. The National Institute for Community Innovations has developed a number of portals that support K-16 reform efforts in educational equity, education technology, K-16 partnership, and data-driven staff development and school change.

One portal that is of critical importance to adult education professionals who train teachers in urban environments is the Urban Teacher Education Portal (http://urban.edreform.net), which provides a clearinghouse of high-quality resources on urban teacher education for use by teacher educators and their K-16 partners. The Digital Equity portal addresses issues of access inequity and it can be found at http://www.digital-equity.org. For educators who are looking for free, high-quality resources to help them address the digital divide in the classroom and community, the Digital Equity Toolkit at http://www.nici-mc2.org/de_toolkit/pages/toolkit.htm can be a great asset.

Another portal that might be of interest to adult education practitioners is the Multimedia Educational Resource for Learning and Online Teaching (MERLOT) site located at http://www.merlot.org. The MERLOT site is designed for faculty and students in higher education. It provides links to online learning materials, with annotations such as peer reviews and assignments.

One of the benefits of a portal is that anyone may use it as enrichment for courses, study groups, and research. Experts in the field review portal materials based on relevance, quality, basis in research, and significant contribution to the field (Conceição, Sherry, Gibson, and Amenta-Shin, 2003). Adult education practitioners can take advantage of these resources to learn about topics related to the digital divide. One limitation for the field of adult education is that there is not a portal addressing issues specific to adult education research and practice and the digital divide.

Conclusion

It is important that educators of adults be aware of the factors and obstacles that limit access and usage of information technology by adults. Statistics show that use of information technology by adults in an urban setting is a product of access. Data indicate that there are cultural differences in how information technology is perceived by different racial or ethnic groups. Because poverty also affects the digital divide, these issues take on special significance in the urban environment because of the central city's diverse composition. Realizing both the urban location and cultural factors that lead to access, the educator of urban adults has a more precise understanding of the issues that make up this potentially dangerous inequity.

Like urban location and cultural factors, literacy has an effect on access and use of information technology by adults. Language and digital literacy are critical elements of the digital divide. As a result of deficits in Internet content, educators of urban adults need to be versed in the culture they serve and knowledgeable about current pertinent local information (Cassara, 1990). Online instructional tools might also need to be reassessed in regard to better serving their target demographic. Community links, community profiles, and forums for expression of local participants' views could serve to enhance formal, nonformal, and informal learning.

References

Bullard, R. D., Johnson, G. S., and Torres, A. O. "Race, Equity, and Smart Growth: Why People of Color Must Speak for Themselves." Atlanta: Environmental Justice Resource Center [http://www.ejrc.cau.edu/raceequitysmartgrowth.htm#aa%20concentrations], 2000.

Cassara, B. B. *Adult Education in a Multicultural Society.* New York: Routledge, 1990.

Coley, R. J., Cradler, J., and Engel, P. K. Computers and Classrooms: The Status of Technology in U.S. Schools. Princeton, N.J.: Educational Testing Services, 1997.

Conceição, S., Sherry, L., Gibson, D., and Amenta-Shin, G. Managing Digital Resources for an Urban Education Portal. Ed-Media Conference Proceedings, Honolulu, Hawaii, June 2003.

Coombs, P. H., Prosser, R. C., and Ahmed, M. New Paths to Learning: For Rural Children and Youth. New York: International Council for Educational Development, 1973.

Danziger, S. K. "Barriers to the Employment of Welfare Recipients." Unpublished manuscript, Madison, Wis., 1999.

De Haymes, M. V., Kilty, K. M., and Segal, E. A. *Latino Poverty in the New Century: Inequalities, Challenges, and Barriers.* New York: Haworth Press, 2000.

Digital Divide Network. Digital Divide Basics Fact Sheet. [http://www.digitaldividenetwork.org/content/stories/index.cfm?key=168], retrieved Oct. 5, 2002.

Duranton, G. *The Economics of Production Systems: Segmentation and Skill-Biased Change.* London: London School of Economics, 2002.

Gilster, P. Digital Literacy. New York: Wiley, 1997.

Graham, S. "Bridging Urban Digital Divides? Urban Polarisation and Information and Communications Technologies (ICTs)." Urban Studies, 2001, 39(1), 33-56.

Groneman, N. "Business Demands for Web-Related Skills as Compared to Other Computer Skills." Delta Pi Epsilon Journal, 2000, 42(4), 207-211.

Harris, L., and Associates. "Bringing a Nation Online: The Importance of Federal Leadership." Report by the Leadership Conference on Civil Rights Education Fund and the Benton Foundation with support from the Ford Foundation. July 2002.

Haymes, S. N. *Race, Culture, and the City: A Pedagogy for Black Urban Struggle.* Albany: State University of New York Press, 1995.

Hoffman, D. L., and Novak, T. P. "Bridging the Digital Divide: The Impact of Race on Computer Access and Internet Use." Science, 1998, 280, 390-391.

Hoffman, D. L., Novak, T. P., Schlosser, A. E. "The Evolution of the Digital Divide: How Gaps in Internet Access May Impact Electronic Commerce." Journal of Computer-Mediated Communication, 2000, 5(3) [http://www.ascusc.org/jcmc/vol5/issue3/hoffman.html].

Hoffman, D. L., Novak, T. P., and Venkatesh, A. "Diversity on the Internet: The Relationship of Race to Access and Usage." In A. Garmer (ed.), *Investigating in Diversity: Advancing Opportunities for Minorities and the Media.* Washington, D.C.: Aspen Institute, 1997.

Ingle, H. T. Connections Across Culture, Demography, and New Technologies. In G. Solomon, N. Allen, and P. Resta (eds.), *Toward Digital Equity: Bridging the Divide in Education.* Upper Saddle River, N.J.: Allyn and Bacon, 2002.

Kolko, B. E., Nakamura, L., and Rodman, G. B. (eds.). *Race in Cyberspace*. New York: Routledge, 2000.

Kominski, R. Computer Use in the United States: The Bureau of Census Surveys. Paper presented at annual meeting of the American Society for Information Science. Washington D. C.: U.S. Bureau of the Census, 1992.

Lazarus, W., and Mora, F. Online Content for Low-Income and Underserved Americans: The Digital Divide's New Frontiers. Santa Monica, Calif.: Children's Partnership [http://www.childrenspartnership.org/pub/low_income/low_income.pdf], 2000.

Levine, D. World Population Counter. [http://www.ibiblio.org/lunarbin/worldpop], retrieved Mar. 2002.

Merriam, S. B., and Caffarella, R. S. *Learning in Adulthood: A Comprehensive Guide*. (2nd ed.) San Francisco: Jossey-Bass, 1999.

Mineta, N. Y. Falling Through the Net: Toward Digital Inclusion. Washington, D.C.: U.S. Department of Commerce, Economics and Statistics Administration, National Telecommunications and Information Administration, 2000.

National Adult Literacy Database, Bridging the Gap Between Literacy and Technology. New Brunswick, Canada: National Adult Literacy Database [http://www.nald.ca/CLR/Btg/BTGHomePage/HomePage.htm], 2000.

National Center for Education Statistics. Defining and Measuring Literacy Washington, D.C.: National Center for Education Statistics[http://nces.ed.gov/naal/defining/defining.asp], retrieved May 5, 2003.

Newburger, E. C. Computer Use in the United States: Population Characteristics (Special Report No. P20-522). Washington D.C.: U.S. Census Bureau, 1997.

Newburger, E. C. Home Computers and Internet Use in the United States: August 2000. (Special Report no. P23-207) Washington D.C.: U.S. Census Bureau, 2001.

Proctor, B. D., and Dalaker, J. Poverty in the United States: 2001. Washington, D.C.: U.S. Census Bureau, 2002.

Rainie, L., and Packel, D. "The Changing Online Population: It's More and More Like the General Population." In More Online, Doing More. Washington, D.C.: Pew Internet and American Life Project [http://www.pewinternet.org/reports/pdfs/PIP_Changing_Population.pdf], Feb. 18, 2001.

Richardson, K., Spears, D., and Richards, M. *Race, Culture and Intelligence*. Harmondsworth: Penguin 1972.

Rocap, K. "Defining and Designing Literacy for the Twenty-First Century." In G. Solomon, N. Allen, and P. Resta (eds.), *Toward Digital Equity: Bridging the Divide in Education*. Upper Saddle River, N.J.: Allyn & Bacon, 2002.

Samovar, L. A., and Porter, R. E. *Intercultural Communication: A Reader*. Belmont, Calif.: Wadsworth, 1972.

Spooner, T. Asian-Americans and the Internet: The Young and the Connected. Washington, D.C.: Pew Internet Project, 2001.

Spooner, T., and Rainie, L. Hispanic/Latinos and the Internet. Washington, D.C.: Pew Internet & American Life, 2001.

U. S. Census Bureau. (2000). Compariablity of current population survey incomes data with other data. Washington, D.C.: U.S. Census Bureau, 2000. [http://www.census.gov/hhes/www/income/compare1.html], retrieved Apr. 7 2002.

U.S. Census Bureau. "Urban and Rural Definitions." [http://www.census.gov/population/censusdata/urdef.txt], Oct. 1995.

U.S. Census Bureau. "Comparability of Current Population Survey Incomes Data with Other Data" [http://www.census.gov/hhes/www/income/compare1.html], retrieved Apr. 7, 2002.

United States Congress. House Committee on Small Business. Subcommittee on Empowerment. (2001). The digital divide: field hearing before the Subcommittee on Empowerment of the Committee on Small Business, One Hundred Sixth Congress, second session, Carson, CA, April 25, 2000. Washington: U.S. G.P.O.: For sale by the U.S. G.P.O. Supt. of Docs. Congressional Sales Office.

U.S. Department of Commerce, National Telecommunications and Information Administration. Falling Through the Net II: New Data on the Digital Divide. Washington, D.C., 1998.

Webster's II New College Dictionary. Houghton Mifflin, 1999.

Wiburg, K. M., and Butler, J. F. "Creating Educational Access." In G. Solomon, N. Allen, and P. Resta (eds.), *Toward Digital Equity: Bridging the Divide in Education.* Upper Saddle River, N.J.: Allyn & Bacon, 2002.

Yu, P. K. "Bridging the Digital Divide: Equality in the Information Age." Cardozo Arts & Entertainment Law Journal, 2002, 20(1), 1-52.

Zgoda, K. "The Space Between: An Interview with CTCNet Executive Director Karen Chandler." Community Technology Review, Winter-Spring 2002.

DANIEL T. NORRIS is a doctoral student in the Adult and Continuing Education Program at the University of Wisconsin-Milwaukee.

SIMONE CONCEÇÃO is assistant professor of adult education and technology in the University of Wisconsin-Milwaukee's Department of Administrative Leadership.

7

The urban context generates a barrage of disorienting dilemmas for urban learners, thereby complicating and challenging the promotion of transformative learning.

Transformative Learning and the Urban Context

Patricia Leong Kappel, Barbara J. Daley

The role of transformative learning in adult learning and development has received much attention since transformational theory was introduced by Mezirow in 1978 (Taylor, 1997). Transformative learning theory emerged during a period of escalating growth in adult education. It is unique to adulthood, for it addresses the phenomenon of adult learning from the perspective of adult characteristics and adult social roles, responsibilities, and experiences (Stein, 2000). Simple learning, as well as the elaboration of existing paradigms and systems of thinking, feeling, or doing, proved insufficient on its own in assisting adults to negotiate lives made increasingly complex by modern society. As a result, transformational theory has become the most developed theory in adult education in its concentration on a trait exclusive to adult learners: the ability to reflect critically on experiences, integrate this knowledge into existing knowledge structures, and take action on these insights. Transformative learning is seen as a way to help adults make sense of their experiences and make meaning of and put balance into their lives. It can enhance the ability of adults to become self-directed and to act upon assumptions and premises on which their performance, achievement, and productivity are based (Merriam and Caffarella, 1999).

Studies on transformative learning in educational settings are scant, however. Taylor (1997) reviewed published studies that followed Mezirow's (1981) introduction of his theory. Of the thirty-nine studies on transformational learning, with topics ranging from health to cultural assimilation to unemployment to domestic abuse, only four were situated in educational settings. Of these four, none were in the context of the urban setting.

The purpose of this chapter, therefore, is to add to the knowledge of transformative learning by exploring its application in the urban context. First, we outline the theory's basic assumptions as well as the expanded perspectives on transformational learning. Next, we present a profile of the urban adult learner and compare it to the assumptions of transformational learning theory. Finally, in a discussion of implications for practice, we identify elements necessary for facilitating the transformative learning of urban adult populations.

Mezirow's Transformational Learning Theory

Transformative learning theory describes how learners construe, validate, and reformulate the meaning of their experiences. From these meaning schemes—specific beliefs, attitudes, assumptions, and emotional reactions—individuals build meaning structures, which guide their responses and actions. However, these meaning structures undergo change when new knowledge or experience is integrated into the structures. This change results from a disorienting dilemma, which can be triggered by a life crisis, a major life transition, or an accumulation of transformation in meaning schemes over time (Imel, 1998; Mezirow, 1991). This disorienting dilemma occurs when individuals discover that their former ways of responding are ineffective (Merriam and Caffarella, 1991). Deconstruction of meaning structures occurs during the process of critical reflection, a significant aspect of transformative learning. During this process, individuals conduct a self-examination and reassess their orientation to perceiving, knowing, believing, feeling, and acting and critique the presuppositions on which these aspects are built (Mezirow, 1990, 1994). On the basis of this examination, perspective transformation can occur, which is "a process of becoming critically aware of how and why our presuppositions have come to constrain the way we perceive, understand, and feel about our world; changing these structures of habitual expectations to make possible a more inclusive, discriminating, and integrating perspective; and finally, making choices or otherwise acting upon these new understandings" (Mezirow, 1990, p.14).

In summary, transformative learning results from perspective transformation, from which, through critical reflection on assumptions and beliefs, new frames of reference (meaning structures) emerge. Through discourse, validation of these new meanings completes the process and creates new lenses from which individuals can view and make sense of their worlds (Mezirow, 1997a, 1997b).

Expanded Perspectives on Transformational Theory

Transformative learning's importance to adult learning development is not debated in the literature. Scholars recognize that disorienting dilemmas are inherent to adult life in modern society, where individuals attempt to navigate through the complexities of life and fight to maintain balance amid their multiple and sometimes conflicting life roles. Their struggle raises questions, however, about Mezirow's theoretical perspective. Its scope has been criticized by scholars who argue in favor of a more holistic perspective on the individual in relationship to the transformative process.

Deemphasizing Rationalism. Mezirow (1981, 1991) is perceived by some scholars as too rationalistic and is criticized for his attempts to systematize the areas of distortion that require transformation without directly criticizing the current economic, social, and political factors inherently tied to these distortions (Merriam and Caffarella, 1991). Taylor (1997) also criticizes the theory for its overemphasis on critical reflection, a process that he regards as too rational and limiting due to its autonomous and self-directed nature. This emphasis on exclusive meaning-making contradicts the adult learning need for connectedness, required in areas such as interpersonal and communication skill development. Moreover, the need for validation of meaning, a step in the process of perspective transformation, necessitates discourse, for as Cochrane (1981, p. 114) says, "It is in and through the disclosure of one's self to another that meaning develops and is enhanced." In addition, Mezirow's orientation toward autonomy is seen to reflect uncritically the values of the dominant culture in our society—a culture that is masculine, white, and middle class (Merriam and Caffarella, 1991).

A More Holistic Perspective. Supporting the deemphasis on rationalism is Boyd's (Dirkx, 2000) psychological perspective on transformative learning, in which he asserts that emotional and spiritual dimensions also enter into this journey toward self-discovery. He grounds his view in Jung's (Dirkx, 2000) concept of individuation: a process of forming and differentiating individuals, with the goal of developing the individual personality. The individual is considered a composite of multiple selves, with the conscious, more rational self as a less than dominant factor in a person's development. According to this concept, the forces of individuation are unconscious and are manifested within affective, emotional, and spiritual dimensions (Dirkx, 2000). Transformative learning, from Boyd's view, results in a "fundamental change in one's personality, involving the resolution of personal dilemma and the expansion of consciousness resulting in greater personality integration" (Boyd, 1989, p. 459). Studies have shown the significance of intuition, affective learning, extrarational influences, the guiding force of emotions, and relationships in this process (Taylor, 1997). Imagination, images, and symbols also work in the creation of meaning in this development of a deeper understanding of the self and one's relationship with the world (Dirkx, 2000).

The Importance of Context. Context reflects the sociocultural and personal factors that affect the process of transformative learning. These factors include the immediate environment of the learning event as well as what the individual brings to the learning situation: a unique context composed of a familial and social history and an individual orientation, which includes readiness for change, experience, prior stressful life events, and a predisposition for transformative experience (Taylor, 1997). Taylor sees context as a critical factor in the process of transformative learning and criticizes Mezirow for not linking the construction of knowledge with the context of learning and with what the learner brings to the event. Taylor contends that this linkage needs to be located in the learner's relationships with others, which further supports the premise that transformative learning is a socially grounded rather than a solitary activity.

The Urban Adult Learner in Context. Examining transformative learning in an urban context necessitates an understanding of what we mean by urban (see Chapter One of this volume). For our purposes here, "the principal features by which we define and focus our discussion of urban are density and diversity, and their consequences: anonymity and complexity" (Daley, Fisher, and Martin, 2000, p. 540). For many urban learners, anonymity is the consequence of political, social, and economic barriers that prevent the development of sustained relationships and restrict access to urban power structures and resources. Complexity is inherent in the lives of urban learners and is manifested in the multiple stressors created by the environment of urban poverty, violence, illiteracy, and unemployment.

The individuals in the following examples were participants enrolled in training programs sponsored by their welfare-reform agencies and facilitated by one of the authors at a Midwest urban vocational technical college. These cases illustrate how anonymity and complexity factor into the ceaseless struggle of urban learners to reconcile disorienting dilemmas to tenuously constructed meaning schemes. They confirm the complications of transformational theory in the urban context and identify implications for practice in working with urban adult populations.

Johnnie

Johnnie is a forty-seven-year-old African American widowed mother of four children. When her youngest child reaches the age of eighteen in the near future, Johnnie will forfeit the county's monetary support on which she has relied since losing her assembly job two years ago. She has a reading disability that challenges her unwavering pursuit of a GED, a requirement for the culinary arts apprenticeship she is seeking. Johnnie is also guardian, however, to her schizophrenic adult son, who, when not on medication and high on illegal drugs, is prone to violence. She has missed GED class time and some culinary training days due to exhaustion from sleepless nights spent on guard against the unpredictable behaviors of her son, who has been living with her. His two recent physical attacks on his mother forced Johnnie to wrangle with the police and the legal and health care systems to obtain a restraining order and to secure a mental health care facility that would accept her son. This was not the first episode of this nature involving her son; there have been several in the past year. Her voice ached in frustration as she sighed, "I am so tired. Sometimes I just want to give up, but I can't, even if I want to. I'm just so tired."

For now, however, Johnnie's outlook has improved. With her son finally in residence at a mental health facility, Johnnie has been freed to concentrate on herself. She is thrilled with her new part-time job, where she can apply her culinary skills in the kitchen of a day care center. During her off hours, Johnnie continues to pursue her literacy goals at a community-based organization.

Darren

Thirty-one-year-old Darren, an African American single parent, admitted to a "wilder" life in his youth, but when he assumed custody of his son (now twelve years old) more than ten years ago, those wild days were gone. An interest in cooking led Darren eventually to become lead cook at a chain restaurant where he was employed for more than three years. A serious attack on the street, however, resulted in the loss of an eye and the loss of his job. He turned to a county agency for assistance until he could "get back on my feet." Darren has been a model student (he earned an A) in his culinary arts class at the city's vocational-technical school where he volunteers time to assist his instructor in his other classes and activities. When asked his opinion of his culinary class and the instructor, Darren responded, "This is the only place where I am happy. Out there, it's not good, but here, … it's safe. I like being here. Mr. P [the instructor] … he's cool. He lets me do my own thing. He's really cool."

Unfortunately, Darren suffered a temporary setback recently when his home was burglarized. This event reinforced his concern about his neighborhood and its negative influences on his son. "It [the flat] was all I could find and afford, but I'm gonna get us out of there. I don't want to be another statistic… Ya know what I mean?" Darren's son, however, has become the statistic: he was recently arrested for strong-armed robbery.

Linda

Linda, a thirty-five-year-old Native American single mother of three sons participated in a pharmacy technician training program sponsored by her welfare agency and conducted at the city's vocational-technical college. Although an incomplete English requirement prevented her from obtaining her certificate, a large chain drug store two blocks from her home hired her as a cashier and offered her the opportunity to obtain the pharmacy technician certificate she had just missed acquiring. Linda was preparing for the exam when her flat was destroyed by fire. Though homeless, she did not qualify for emergency shelter because, she was told, her situation "wasn't severe enough." Living temporarily with her only relation, her estranged father, was not working out. However, because Linda was now employed and "independent," she was not eligible for any kind of assistance from her former welfare agency. As a result, she struggled for two months before finally finding a new residence. Her new home is five miles from where she used to live, necessitating a long commute on the bus to her job. The move also required the transfer of her sons to new schools and finding new day care providers for her children when they are not in school. These arrangements meant lost wages from her $7.85-per-hour job, making her paycheck-to-paycheck existence even more desperate. Linda had the strength to sever herself from an abusive relationship two years ago during the pharmacy technician training, but the problems that have recently arisen seem to have defeated her. Distracted from concentrating on her certification exam, she foresaw the loss of her opportunity for advancement as she tearfully stated, "I'm gonna fail for sure. I just can't concentrate."

Nathan

After completing his state certification in culinary arts, thirty-one-year-old Nathan dropped out of his GED class. He was unable to focus. He was distracted from his GED work by his inability to secure employment and to comply with court orders to make child support payments. Perhaps his sporadic work history or his misdemeanor record had hampered his ability to gain employment. Whatever the reason, Nathan now has to earn money, so using the skills learned from a previous training, he runs his own business as a handyman. Recently, however, Nathan was in the process of reenrolling in GED classes. Prompted by a television advertisement on a particular college, Nathan has decided that he now wants to attend college, but he needs to obtain his GED credential first.

When asked the reason for his sudden interest in returning to his GED pursuits and attending college, Nathan countered by saying, "It wasn't so sudden. I just decided I have to do something with my life." When pressed for a more specific reason for this renewed focus, he responded that there was no thunderbolt that reignited his pursuits. "It was kind of a lot of things. Mainly, I was seeing too many of my friends going nowhere, and too many of them dying." He added, "But if it weren't for this program and the people here, I wouldn't have come even this far."

Disorienting Dilemmas in the Urban Context

What do these vignettes of urban learners tell us? As indicated in Table 7.1, the urban context often acts as a multilayered web of disorienting and intersecting dilemmas. These dilemmas can make learning challenging for urban learners, but they can also contribute to the learners' desire, motivation, and frustration with the process. The vignettes are laced with examples of disorienting dilemmas that arise from the anonymity and complexity of urban life. However, anonymity and complexity have varied outcomes for different urban learners, leading to idiosyncratic changes in meaning schemes. These vignettes demonstrate how the disorienting dilemmas in the lives of urban learners prompt the process of critical reflection and a change in

Table 7.1: Transformational Theory and the Urban Learner

Learner	Original Meaning Scheme	Disorienting Dilemma	Transformative Learning and New Meaning Scheme	Practice Implications and Interventions
Johnnie	Goals are attainable as long as one works hard	Unemployment	Unpredictable life circumstances can thwart even the most dedicated efforts	Listen and support
	Financial assistance will be available	Losing financial assistance	Goal achievement requires persistence	Give guidance in problem solving
		Schizophrenic son	Self-reliance leads to more stable financial situation	Consider need to accommodate learners going through crises
Darren	Financial independence can fulfill dreams	Street attack	Goal attainment may encounter challenges and delays	Allow adults to be independent decision makers and self-directed learners
	Individuals can control own destiny	Loss of job	View strengthened that individuals can determine own fate, but others can play important role as well	Create learning environments where learners feelsafe and respected
		Home burglarized		
Linda	Doing as expected and adhering to mandates will result in improved quality of life and independence	Fire and homelessness	Defeat, hopelessness, "Why me?" attitude, disillusionment, feelings of victimization	Support and encourage
		Move/logistical complications	Achieving and maintaining self-reliance may encounter disproportionate share of sabotaging influences	Accommodate and be flexible
		Lack of support		Adopt learner-centered approaches
		Demands of young children		
		Poverty		
Nathan	Accept predetermined life circumstances	Inability to find employment	Renewed educational efforts	Promote life view beyond immediate circumstances
	Goals or direction in life are optional	Court-ordered child support	Learned to value different life outcomes from those of friends	Assist with goal setting
		Loss of friends	Became proactive instead of passive	

meaning schemes. For example, the prospect of losing county support payments pressured Johnnie toward efforts to attain self-sufficiency. However, her struggles with a mentally ill son intensified the pressure, overwhelming her to the point of giving up. Ultimately, Johnnie's meaning scheme changed so that she learned to persist rather than give up. Darren, who lost his job after an attack on the street, set a goal to move to a different environment. Darren's meaning scheme was reinforced when he discovered that he could determine his own fate. Yet his worldview altered with the acceptance of the assistance of others to meet his goals. Conversely, the complexity in Linda's life and her anonymity as a needy individual sabotaged an opportunity to improve her circumstances. Linda learned a hard lesson, that life can dole out its share of misfortune, despite how concerted one's efforts are to succeed. Finally, Nathan, with no job and with court-ordered child support, was tired of seeing his friends die and wanted education to be his key to a better life. Nathan's meaning scheme was transformed when he decided to assume control of his life. By renewing his educational efforts and establishing goals, he showed that he valued life outcomes different from those of his friends.

The urban context generates a barrage of disorienting dilemmas for urban learners, thereby complicating and challenging the promotion of transformative learning. For example, urban learners often reside in geographically concentrated areas of poverty, unemployment, and high crime, as in the case of Darren. Urban families such as Linda's barely survive on wages that are at or below poverty level (Davis-Harrison, 2002). Urban poverty populations also tend to have low labor-market attachment and low educational achievement, and they tend to personify urban complexity in socially reproved behaviors and in the circumstances of welfare dependency, drug use, and single-parent households (Tietz and Chapple, 1998). As illustrated by Linda's situation, some individuals embark but later stumble on the path toward self-sufficiency. The path is illusionary, for the entrapment of poverty and the forces of urban complexity and anonymity alter the course, forcing it to circle endlessly and progress nowhere while defeating will.

In addition, the individual of the central city often has a "split identity," created and fragmented among a large and open set of what Daley, Fisher, and Martin (2000) refer to as discourse communities, which are formed from the relationships the individual has with various facets of her or his environment, such as family, relationships, work, church, and governmental agencies, through which the individual weaves in and out. These communities define knowledge and mold identity, thereby limiting the development of the individual's self-directedness. As demonstrated by Johnnie, Linda, and Darren, the demands of multiple communities not only fragment identity, they also fragment focus. As a result, the individual is challenged to maintain equilibrium while attempting to identify and respond to the most urgent demand from the cacophony of stress-creating voices.

Finally, Tietz and Chapple (1998) contend that industrial urbanization destroyed the relationships and social organizations that constitute communities. As a result, the stabilizing influence of family ties, cultural links, status, and a sense of cohesiveness were diminished, and with this loss, the behavioral controls normally exerted by a community. They further hypothesize that the impact of the migration process was a cause of inner-city poverty. The exit of middle-class families from the influx of greater numbers of poor into the city create a density of people that produces anonymity as a consequence (Daley, Fisher, and Martin, 2000). As seen with the learners previously described, outside of the nuclear family, neither Johnnie, Nathan, Darren, nor Linda had any permanent, significant, personal connections to anyone before their involvement in the community college programs.

The Transformational Urban Adult Learner

In analyzing the urban context and the urban learner, we see the importance of transformative learning in assisting individuals to deal with the unpredictable course of life. As their environment and their relationships with that environment change, adults are forced to adapt to these shifts in order to maintain balance. This necessitates a continual process of reassessment of and modifications to the meaning structures that guide their responses and actions. For many inner-city adults, this is a formidable challenge: to assess their lives critically at multiple junctures in an environment, whose incessant assaults threaten already fragile frames of reference and existence. This challenge mandates a facilitating response from practitioners in adult education: the establishment of transformative learning environments that facilitate perspective transformation. This effort should be grounded, however, in an expanded perspective of Mezirow's Transformational Theory, to include the extrarational factors of the individual and the process of learning.

The Significance of Relationships

Of the thirty-nine transformational learning studies examined by Taylor, the significance of relationships in perspective transformation emerged more frequently than any other factor. In their contradiction of the self-directed nature of Mezirow's assumptions of learning, relationships emphasize the social learning inherent in his constructivist theory. Learning is a complex, continuous cultural process (Buch, 1999) in which individuals seek validation of their meaning structures, causing them to reflect on and interpret the context on which they must base their actions and responses. Within such relationships and interactions, individuals develop connected ways of knowing, defined as learning through relationships. More important, individuals can receive affirming support from the trust and friendship that a collaborative learning process can create (Taylor, 1997). Supportive relationships therefore are key to the transformative learning of urban adults—the necessary learning for inner-city survival. As indicated in Table 7.1, the practice implications for urban adult learners are derived from an understanding of the role that relationships play in the learning process. To deal with the disorienting dilemmas created by the anonymity and complexity in their lives, urban adult learners need solid nurturing relationships that will support their decision making, their problem solving, and the development of a long-term life plan (see Table 7.1 for specific interventions). For example, once Darren felt safe and confident in his relationship with his instructor, he learned that he could achieve his goal of moving to a different neighborhood.

In his expansion of transformational theory, Robertson (1996) promotes a holistic perspective on understanding the individual in relationship to transformative learning. He identifies educational helping relationships as one of four factors significant to the process of perspective transformation. (The others are affective learning, or the guiding role of emotions and feelings in critical reflection; nonconscious learning, or unconscious knowing, the learning that takes place outside of one's focal awareness; and the collective unconscious, where perspectives transcend an egocentric orientation to include those of others.) Robertson (1996), in citing Belenky, Clinchy, Goldberger, and Tarule (1986); Brookfield (1990); and Daloz (1986), describes transformative learning as "a complicated, intensely emotional process that takes considerable skill and knowledge to facilitate effectively and responsibly" (1996, p. 45). Coupled with the complexities and urgencies of the urban learner's impoverished, inner-city life, the professional and ethical implications for practitioners to facilitate the creation of educational helping relationships are clear.

Educational helping relationships call for adult education practitioners to be "facilitators of learning rather than disseminators of knowledge" (Robertson, 1996, p. 42). This helping relationship directs practitioners to assist learners in constructing their own personal knowledge. Even Mezirow joins the promotion of relationships to his generation of new paradigms in his description of andragogy, which calls on practitioners to help adults elaborate, create, and transform their meaning schemes through reflection (Mezirow, 1978, 1991, as cited by Robertson, 1996). Similar to Taylor's descriptions of significant relationships, Robertson's helping relationship is based on trust of the instructor by the learner and care for the learner by the instructor. Goldstein (1999) supports this type of relationship in her assertion that relational factors aid in the co-construction of the intellect, and that affect, volition, and relationships play as critical a role as cognitive factors in the learning process.

A Moral-Ethical Approach to Urban Adult Education

In our experience in working with inner-city learners, educational helping and supportive relationships have been key to facilitating transformative learning, thus fostering the learner's persistence and individual sustenance. Darren's positive regard for his instructor and for his culinary arts class is indicative of an affirming relationship and a learning environment created by the instructor that assists him with sorting through complicating discourses to prioritize his goals. Johnnie's and Linda's personal struggles relate the affective needs of individuals that must be considerations of the learning context if learners are to transform perspectives. Nathan's aspirations to continue his education were rooted in his ties with supportive others, which points to the role of educators in scaffolding learners as they strive toward transformation.

These examples support the stance of Taylor (1997, 1998), Robertson (1996), Boyd (1989), and others that the reliance on rationalism in Mezirow's (1981) transformational theory isolates only one aspect of a learner, whose multiple experiences of past and present elicit more than just a rational response. This individual is a unique composite of multiple influences from her or his environment, and to limit this person's reservoir for response to just the rational part of her or his being neglects the complexity of factors and affects the process that determines that response. For the urban learner who is subject to the intense, barraging, and competing discourses of her or his urban environment, the challenge of sorting through the imperatives to identify the most critical demands is in itself a monumental task. However, when factoring in the survival consequences of these decisions in light of the distracting and debilitating impact of personal crises, the urban adult needs more than theory to guide her or him toward resolution.

If adult education is serious about its quest to establish purpose and about its role in servicing adult learners, then it must be vigilant in critically reflecting on itself by continuing to question and investigate theories that drive practice. Moreover, adult education needs to examine critically current practice in urban programs, to ensure that educational helping relationships are facilitated in environments of trust and support to develop transformative learners. Paramount, however, is the professional and ethical imperative for urban adult education to be proactive in its search for opportunities to address the holistic needs of the most desperate of adult education's learning population.

References

Belenky, M. F., Clinchy, B. M., Goldberger, N. R., and Tarule, J. M. *Women's Ways of Knowing: The Development of Self, Voice, and Mind.* New York: Basic Books, 1986.

Boyd, R. D. "Facilitating Personal Transformation in Small Groups, Part One." *Small Group Behavior,* 1989, 20, 459-474.

Brookfield, S. D. *The Skillful Teacher: On Technique, Trust, and Responsiveness in the Classroom.* San Francisco: Jossey-Bass, 1990.

Buch, A. "Life, Work and Identity: The Mapping of Learning." In T. Challis (ed.), *A First*

International Conference: Researching Work and Learning. Leeds, U.K.: School of Continuing Education, University of Leeds, 1999.

Cochrane, N. J. "The Meanings That Some Adults Derive from Their Personal Withdrawal Experiences: A Dialogical Inquiry." Unpublished doctoral dissertation, University of Toronto, 1981.

Daley, B., Fisher, J. C., and Martin, L. G. "The Urban Context: Examining an Arena for Fostering Adult Education Practice." In A. Wilson and B. Hayes (eds.), *Handbook 2000: Adult and Continuing Education.* San Francisco: Jossey-Bass, 2000.

Daloz, L. A. *Effective Teaching and Mentoring: Realizing the Transformational Power of Adult Learning Experiences.* San Francisco: Jossey-Bass, 1986.

Davis-Harrison, D. "What Has Happened to W-2: Are Participants Transitioning from Welfare to Work?" Presentation conducted at the Planning Responsibly for a Changing Workforce Conference, Milwaukee, Wis., 2002.

Dirkx, J. M. "Transformative Learning and the Journey of Individuation." ERIC Digest, 2000, no. 223 [http://www.ericacve.org/docgen.asp?tbl=digests&ID=108].

Goldstein, L. "The Relational Zone: The Role of Caring Relationships in the Co-construction of the Mind." American Educational Research Journal, 1999, 36, 647-673.

Imel, S. "Transformative Learning in Adulthood." ERIC Digest, no. 200, 1998 [http://www.ericacve.org/docgen.asp?tbl=digests&ID=53].

Mezirow, J. "A Critical Theory of Adult Learning and Education." Adult Education, 1981, 32(1), 3-24.

Mezirow, J. *Fostering Critical Reflection in Adulthood.* San Francisco: Jossey-Bass, 1990.

Mezirow, J. *Transformative Dimensions of Adult Learning.* San Francisco: Jossey-Bass, 1991.

Mezirow, J. "Understanding Transformation Theory." Adult Education Quarterly, 1994, 44(4), 222-232.

Mezirow, J. "Transformation Theory Out of Context." Adult Education Quarterly, 1997a, 48(1), 60-62.

Mezirow, J. "Transformative Learning: Theory to Practice." In P. Cranton (ed.), Transformative Learning in Action: Insights from Practice. New Directions for Adult and Continuing Education, no. 74. San Francisco: Jossey-Bass, 1997b.

Merriam, S. B., and Caffarella, R. S. *Learning in Adulthood.* San Francisco: Jossey-Bass, 1991.

Merriam, S. B., and Caffarella, R. S. *Learning in Adulthood.* (2nd ed.) San Francisco: Jossey-Bass, 1999.

Robertson, D. "Facilitating Transformative Learning: Attending to the Dynamics of the Educational Helping Relationship." Adult Education Quarterly, 1996, 47(1), 41-53.

Stein, D. "Teaching Critical Reflection." Myths and Realities, no. 7, 2000 [http://www.ericacve.org/docgen.asp?tbl=mr&ID=98].

Taylor, E. "Building Upon the Theoretical Debate: A Critical Review of the Empirical Studies of Mezirow's Transformative Learning Theory." Adult Education Quarterly, 1997, 48(1), 34-59.

Taylor, E. W. The Theory and Practice of Transformative Learning: A Critical Review. Columbus, Ohio: Ohio State University, College of Education, Center on Education and Training for Employment, 1998.

Tietz, M., and Chapple, K. "The Causes of Inner-City Poverty: Eight Hypotheses in Search of Reality." Cityscape: A Journal of Policy Development and Research, 1998, 3(3), 33-70.

PATRICIA LEONG KAPPEL is Wisconsin Works projects coordinator at Milwaukee Area Technical College and a doctoral student in the School of Education at the University of Wisconsin-Milwaukee.

BARBARA J. DALEY is associate professor of adult and continuing education at the University of Wisconsin-Milwaukee.

In this volume several themes have emerged regarding the role of urban adult education in assisting residents of inner-city communities to traverse the social, structural, economic, cultural, and technological borders that disconnect them from the more affluent communities in urban areas. These themes also suggest, however, several challenges that remain to be addressed.

New Directions for Urban Adult Education

Larry G. Martin, Elice E. Rogers

A review of the literature on urban education reveals that the urban context is considered an important determinant of practice for K-12 teachers and administrators located in urban schools. Several professional journals, such as the Journal of Urban History, the Urban Education Review, Urban Education, and others routinely publish articles that address the research, theory, policy, and practice concerns of K-12 urban professionals. Yet there is a dearth of literature that addresses the issues and concerns faced by adult education professionals in urban communities.

The urban space that often separates learners from those who could assist them is problematic for adult education professionals. For example, it is not uncommon for learners from poor, disenfranchised, racially segregated inner-city communities to rely on educational programs and services that are provided by teachers, administrators, counselors, and other staff who grew up in middle class, predominantly white suburban communities. However, the urban context can also present tremendous opportunities for human intellectual growth, development, and learning, and for individuals and communities to develop their economic potential. In this volume, several themes have emerged regarding the role of urban adult education in assisting the residents of inner-city communities to traverse the social, structural, economic, cultural, and technological borders that disconnect them from the more affluent communities in urban areas. These themes suggest, however, several challenges that remain to be addressed.

First, Larry G. Martin, in Chapter One, observed that as cities and urban areas attempt to become players in the global economy, they will need to discover ways to revitalize neglected low-income neighborhoods. A major challenge facing adult education practitioners is to discover ways to assist city planners and policymakers in seeking a positive outcome to such initiatives via concerted efforts to provide meaningful education and training programs in these communities.

Second, Elice E. Rogers and Catherine A. Hansman, in Chapter Two, have suggested that many of the federal and state policies that affect the provision of educational services and programs to residents of low-income urban communities are inadequate, unclear, and uncoordinated. In the future, educators of adults will be challenged to ensure that relevant policy initiatives are discussed and debated utilizing insight gained from careful policy-related studies conducted by adult education researchers in the interest of expanding opportunities for adult learners.

Third, Tonette S. Rocco and Suzanne J. Gallagher, in Chapter Three, argued that adult education practitioner should deconstruct the dynamics of our program development, management processes, and classroom practices that assist in replicating the social, political, and economic discourse of the dominant group. Given the historical realities of discriminatory behavior in our society, is it realistic to expect adult education practitioners to understand the subtleties and the pervasiveness of discriminatory behavior in the broad urban arena, and the subtle ways we either ignore or contribute to the types of unwarranted discrimination that produces patterns of segregation in housing, neighborhoods, employment, and K-12 schools? Do adult education practitioners have the conviction and courage to challenge discriminatory behavior in their classrooms and in their communities?

Fourth, educators of adults can provide a bridge for residents of disenfranchised low-income communities to compete in the broader urban arena. However, Talmadge C. Guy, in Chapter Four, argues that to accomplish this goal we should promote critical media literacy among educators of adults as an important first step in addressing the complexities and adverse influences of alternative cultural expressions, such as gangsta rap, and alternative language structures on adult learners and adult classrooms. Given the pervasive influence of hip-hop culture on the values, attitudes, and lifestyles of the younger generations of urban residents, adult education practitioners will be increasingly challenged to close the cultural gap that exists between the adult education staff and adult learners via the creation of cultural crossroads. How will they meet this challenge? In addition, E. Paulette Isaac and Martha Strittmatter Tempesta, in Chapter Five, suggest that community-based programs not only meet the educational needs of adult learners, but also empower them to effect change in their communities. These programs may offer one avenue to bridge the cultural gap mentioned in the preceding chapter. They are often the only reliable and consistent resource within the community. How can educators of adults become more knowledgeable about, understanding of, supportive of, and engaged with these programs?

Fifth, there are cultural differences in how information technology is perceived and used by different racial or ethnic groups. Daniel T. Norris and Simone Conceição, in Chapter Six, argue that we must be aware of the factors and obstacles that limit access and usage of information technology by the adult residents of low-income urban communities. The challenge for educators of urban adults is to utilize their cultural knowledge of such residents and their knowledge about current pertinent local information in order to develop more effective online instructional tools that might be employed to serve their learners.

Sixth, Patricia Leong Kappel and Barbara J. Daley, in Chapter Seven, observe that low-income inner-city learners are often subject to intense, barraging, and competing discourses from their urban environment. For these residents, the challenge of sorting through the imperatives in order to prioritize the most critical demands is a monumental task. Can it be that transformative learning theory is inadequate to explain the complex and challenging experiences that routinely confront low-income inner-city residents? A challenge for adult education practitioners is to expand the theory to ensure that our educational helping relationships are facilitated in environments of trust and support to develop transformative learners.

Residents of inner-city communities face numerous context-specific obstacles and barriers in their struggle to acquire quality educational programming that will assist them to develop the economic viability of their communities. In this volume we have attempted to provide insight into the education and learning problems and needs confronted by low-income residents of inner-city communities, and to offer fresh perspectives and approaches to practice that will assist educators of adults to develop culturally responsive adult education programming. It is hoped that a renewed investment in such communities by dedicated adult education practitioners will assist these learners in developing more educational, economical, and social advancement options and choices for themselves and their families.

LARRY G. MARTIN is professor of adult and continuing education at the University of Wisconsin-Milwaukee.

ELICE E. ROGERS is assistant professor of adult learning and development at Cleveland State University.

INDEX

Back Issue/Subscription Order Form

Copy or detach and send to:
Jossey-Bass, A Wiley Imprint, 989 Market Street, San Francisco CA 94103-1741

Call or fax toll-free: Phone 888-378-2537 6:30AM – 3PM PST; Fax 888-481-2665

Back Issues: Please send me the following issues at $29 each
(Important: please include ISBN number with your order.)

_____

_____

_____

$ _____ Total for single issues

$ _____ SHIPPING CHARGES: SURFACE   Domestic Canadian
　　　　　　　　　　　　　　　First Item $5.00 $6.00
　　　　　　　　　　　　　Each Add'l Item $3.00 $1.50
For next-day and second-day delivery rates, call the number listed above.

Subscriptions: Please _start _renew my subscription to *New Directions for Adult and Continuing Education* for the year 2_____at the following rate:

U.S.	_ Individual $80	_ Institutional $160
Canada	_ Individual $80	_ Institutional $200
All Others	_ Individual $104	_ Institutional $234
Online Subscription		_ Institutional $176

**For more information about online subscriptions visit
www.interscience.wiley.com**

$ _____ Total single issues and subscriptions (Add appropriate sales tax for your state for single issue orders. No sales tax for U.S. subscriptions. Canadian residents, add GST for subscriptions and single issues.)

_ Payment enclosed (U.S. check or money order only)
_ VISA _MC _AmEx _# _____ Exp. Date _____

Signature _____ Day Phone _____
_ Bill Me (U.S. institutional orders only. Purchase order required.)

Purchase order # _____
　　　　　　　Federal Tax ID13559302　　　　　　**GST 89102 8052**

Name _____

Address _____

_____

Phone _____ E-mail _____

For more information about Jossey-Bass, visit our Web site at www.josseybass.com

**NEW DIRECTIONS FOR
ADULT AND CONTINUING EDUCATION
IS NOW AVAILABLE ONLINE AT WILEY INTERSCIENCE**

What is Wiley InterScience?

Wiley InterScience is the dynamic online content service from John Wiley & Sons delivering the full text of over 300 leading scientific, technical, medical, and professional journals, plus major reference works, the acclaimed *Current Protocols* laboratory manuals, and even the full text of select Wiley print books online.

What are some special features of Wiley InterScience?

Wiley InterScience Alerts is a service that delivers table of contents via e-mail for any journal available on Wiley InterScience as soon as a new issue is published online.
Early View is Wiley's exclusive service presenting individual articles online as soon as they are ready, even before the release of the compiled print issue. These articles are complete, peer-reviewed, and citable.
CrossRef is the innovative multi-publisher reference linking system enabling readers to move seamlessly from a reference in a journal article to the cited publication, typically located on a different server and published by a different publisher.

How can I access Wiley InterScience?

Visit http://www.interscience.wiley.com

Guest Users can browse Wiley InterScience for unrestricted access to journal Tables of Contents and Article Abstracts, or use the powerful search engine.
Registered Users are provided with a *Personal Home Page* to store and manage customized alerts, searches, and links to favorite journals and articles. Additionally, Registered Users can view free Online Sample Issues and preview selected material from major reference works.
Licensed Customers are entitled to access full-text journal articles in PDF, with select journals also offering full-text HTML.

How do I become an Authorized User?

Authorized Users are individuals authorized by a paying Customer to have access to the journals in Wiley InterScience. For example, a university that subscribes to Wiley journals is considered to be the Customer. Faculty, staff and students authorized by the university to have access to those journals in Wiley InterScience are Authorized Users. Users should contact their Library for information on which Wiley journals they have access to in Wiley InterScience.

ASK YOUR INSTITUTION ABOUT WILEY INTERSCIENCE TODAY!